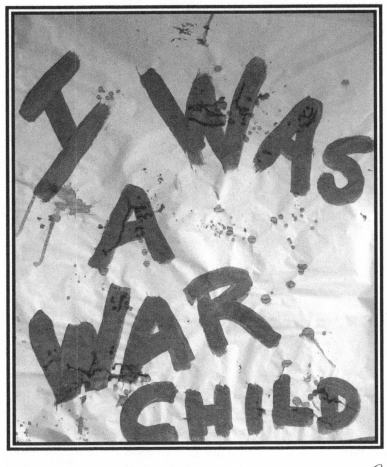

# World War II Memoir of a little French Catholic girl

*The story of a young girl from a large Catholic family struggling to survive during and after the Nazi occupation of France, May 1940–June 1946*

## Hélène Gaillet de Neergaard

ISBN-10: 1499612028
ISBN-13: 978-1499612028
Library of Congress Control Number: 2014909792
CreateSpace Independent Publishing Platform
North Charleston, South Carolina

# BOOKS BY THE AUTHOR

*The Boat Book: A Guide and Reference Book for All Boaters*
*Nautical Terms & Abbreviations: The Language of Boats and Boating*
*Invitation to a Slow Death: The Life of Lifers*
*Chantons Ensemble: Songs of my Youth*

*For Children:*
*Junior goes Sailing*
*Junior goes Ballooning*
*Junior goes Hiking*

To my wonderful parents who salvaged my life
and to my one and only favorite brother,
Bernard Antoine Gaillet,
who helped me write about it

# ACKNOWLEDGMENTS & THANKS TO:

Mokus de Barcza, for all the understanding and admiration;
Anne-Charlotte de Barcza, for all the love and affection;
Rose Brady, for the epilogue;
Valerie Brown, for photo editing;
Nadia Daricekova, for wardrobe;
Peter Evans, for guidance;
Michael Foldes, for Ragazine enlightenment;
Christine Frank, literary agent;
Richard W. Gorman, the catcher of stones;
Bernard and Fanny Guerlain, for memories;
Paul Ingrassia, for leadership;
Gonzague Lemaitre, for genealogy;
Matthew Devitt Lohan, for trusting my talents;
Michael Lohan, for valuable support;
Patrick O'Connor, for editing;
Kathi Paton, literary agent;
Jacqueline Simenauer, literary agent;
Dimitri and Charlotte Stancioff, for memories;
Oliver Stone, for everlasting friendship;
Joseph Szilva, for stability;
Brigitte van den Hove Smith, for language skills;
George P. Walmsley, for website;
My family, for trusting my ability to write our story;
My friends, for their support and patience;
My husband, William Field de Neergaard, for being there.

# TABLE OF CONTENTS

# $\mathscr{P}$HOTOGRAPHS

# $\mathscr{P}$ROLOGUE

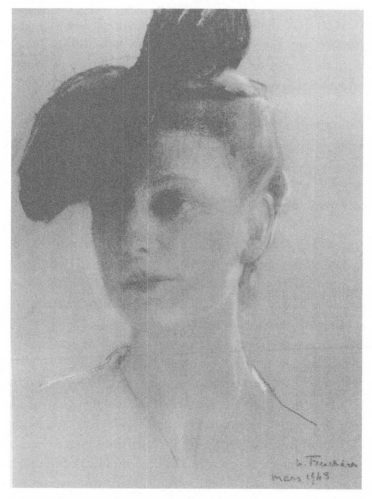

*My Mother Elisabeth Avot Gaillet*

In 1996, my mother died in her sleep at the age of ninety-two.

In her bureau, I found some loose pages written in 1974. She had just turned seventy and had lived in the United States for twenty-eight years. So sad; it was too late to ask her for her memories.

On the threshold of old age, my memories overflow in a panicked disorder. Cocooned in the sadness of all I have lost, worthless, useless, I still feel young. Memories are the only reality, for I have lost all that which shaped my youth and the only success I've ever known, my art gallery. Children, grandchildren help fight the deep despair and hollowness of this life. Souvenirs pierce my heart like a knife and shatter a pleasant day. There is no recourse to this malady. Now and forever adrift, surrounded by foreigners who talk in a difficult language, French is the only language my heart will ever understand. There is no harsher punishment than to always remain a stranger. In a multitude of thoughts and ideas, I remain isolated, a prisoner in a dark cave without sun.
*Elisabeth Avot Gaillet*

Details of the massive exodus forced upon French citizens by the invasion of the Nazis have prompted me to focus on this momentous history from a personal point of view, that of a little Catholic girl in a large family, escaping barely one step ahead of the German army.

It has taken me decades to find the courage to talk about those childhood years, to free my mind and to open my heart to the understanding and forgiveness that I needed to accept before putting pen to paper. My aim with these memoirs is to focus on the dramatic survival of my family and to add more details to the historical perspective of World War II.

In 1972, my father presented his six children with a brown three-ring binder filled with three hundred typewritten pages. These were his memoirs of a war never forgotten. He was the kind of man who would hand us such a personal gift and at the same time never expect any of us to read it. Though often right in his assumptions, this time he was mistaken. Over the years his memoirs have become a family treasure uniquely special to each of us. As I sit to compose my firsthand reflections on this terrible war, I cannot help but connect his experience, so different and adult, with my childish perceptions.

Some of the events I describe are drawn from my father's words in that now faded and tattered brown binder. Some are from stories he told, forever etched in my understanding of the journey that ultimately led us to a long-awaited peace. Every word I write is important, as I am the only witness now able to document the hardships of my family, and my parents' sacrifices and unyielding faith during a time when others chose to lay down and die.

Our family experienced unique tribulations amid the confusion of a country falling apart. My father's cunning, my mother's support, our servants' loyalty, our God's protection, and a great amount of luck kept us alive. In many ways it is miraculous that any of us survived. Certainly mine is not the first, last, or most important account of the tragedies that France and her people endured. It is not my intention to offer solutions to any of the questions that history books have yet to answer. Instead, as I write the story of the Gaillet family to the best of my recollection, from my birth in 1935 until the end of my family's turmoil in 1946, I can only hope that it inspires those who read about these horrors to work for peace.

# PART ONE

# 1

## A BULLET SHATTERS PEACE

t was a miracle none of us was killed when a Nazi bullet ripped through our front door and ricocheted on the marble floor. We'd been hustled to the cellar many times before as sirens blared overhead. We knew where to run for cover when those alarms went off. We had been prisoners indoors for the past several weeks; sirens kept us from sleeping at night and from going to Sunday Mass or to school. We shuffled silently down the thick wooden steps and found our places on two mattresses along the back wall, gathering our blankets for protection. Scared and silent in the darkness of the cool cellar, we waited.

Along the left-hand wall was a haphazard string of chairs padded with cushions, small tables scattered in between. Maman sighed and sat in her armchair with the baby, barely two years old, on her lap, whimpering as if aware of the danger.

"Shh, shh," Maman rocked her absentmindedly, looking around for our shapes, anxious.

"Charlotte? Are you there?" she whispered.

"*Oui*, Maman." Charlotte's voice was clear, almost excited.

"Fanny? And you?"

"*Oui*, Maman," came back, soft as a whisper.

"Zabeth?"

"*Oui, je suis lá*," answered my ever-lively sister.

"Bernard?"

Silence. A little louder, "Bernard?"

"*Il est pas là,*" I said. My voice scared me.

"Oh!"

"He is not here," I whispered to myself, fearful of making noise.

Maman half rose, tightening her grip on the baby, which caused her to howl. Maman soothed her as she called to our butler.

"Arthur! Please!"

Sprightly for a man of his girth, Arthur dashed upstairs, scanning one room after another, finally stumbling onto Bernard standing at an upstairs bathroom window cracked open. Oblivious to danger, bemused and mesmerized, watching fighter planes shooting at each other while antiaircraft shells left wisps of black smoke in an otherwise bright blue sky, my brother was hypnotized by the action in the sky and deafened by the staccato of machine guns.

At that moment, with the family cowering in the reinforced cellar, Maman heard an unexpected clamor coming from the entrance foyer. She heard a shot and crystal shattering on the marble floor.

"There goes the chandelier." She sighed, staring at the baby.

On the way back to the cellar, Bernard found the bullet that had pierced the front door and ricocheted in the entry hall. The war was on our doorstep. Heavy banging warned us of troops outside, but no one moved. Papa was gone on some urgent business, and his warning rang in our ears: "If the Germans arrive, *don't open the door.* HIDE!"

# 2

# ℐMMINENT ᴅANGER

*Mimi Gaillet — deux ans*

My father, Émile Pierre Gaillet, in 1906. Nicknamed Mimi until he was four years old,
he was dressed as a girl for most of those years. When he was four and starting school, his
mother relented and had his long curls cut off. He was her fourth boy, and she was desperate
to have a girl, just the reverse of what happened in my family; I should have been a boy.

*P*apa was born in March 1904 near Roubaix, Maman in January of the same year in St. Omer, only seventy-five kilometers apart. She loved to brag she was older, but there was never any doubt that Papa ran the show. Having barely survived Word War I as an adolescent, he was well acquainted with the catastrophic fluctuations of war.

In 1914, while his father and three older brothers fought in the trenches, mother and ten-year-old son aimlessly wandered the country-side. They evaded enemy bombardments by hiding in abandoned farms, half-starved and riddled with fear. Papa never forgot seeing the mangled faces of his countrymen, their eyes vacant in thousand-yard stares, bodies bloated with decay, their blue faces caught with shock in the thunderous roars of explosions. They finally returned home at war's end in 1918, when Papa was fourteen years old. Miraculously, his father and brothers had survived.

In 1939, aware of the rumblings of war, Papa was hell-bent to shield his own family from the kind of atrocities he had witnessed as a young boy. He promised himself and God that his wife would never have to feel what his mother did. He wanted to ensure that his children would weather this hell untarnished and retain their innocence. He would send them wherever he could, however he could, to stave off a malady that he could never wash off himself. Thus, he began preparations for a quick evacuation should France be attacked, which he thought was imminent.

Once Belgian King Leopold III surrendered, Hitler sent his troops marching through Belgium on May 10, 1940, entering France through a totally unguarded border. It was the day after Papa had left us to get a small Peugeot pickup truck in the suburbs; all of his company's trucks had been requisitioned for the war effort. That is the day our house got hit, the day we hid in the cellar while Nazis pounded on our front door.

# 3

## CONFUSION AND DISARRAY

*I*n the summer and fall of 1939, only thirty-five, the father of six children, and the head of a household that numbered eleven people, Papa anticipated Hitler's intentions toward France. He sensed, he *knew*, rattling in his bones, that another war was coming. The proximity of his home to the Belgian border, where Hitler was marauding, was of profound concern.

Some months before, Papa had ordered a small Peugeot pickup truck, and had a trailer built that could be towed behind the family car. He had asked his wife to gather nonperishable products and stack them in the basement: rice, flour, sugar, lentils, dried peas, coffee, to which were added pots and pans and other things that he hoped would help us survive the coming war.

On May 9, he left us to get the truck. When he arrived, he was upset that the truck would not be ready until the next day. He got in touch with a couple of family members who lived nearby. They were standing in the town square, smoking, when suddenly a siren started blaring above them, jolting the cigarettes from their mouths and fingers.

"God, here we go," Uncle Paul said as they dashed into the cellar of the nearer of two cafés that faced each other across a gurgling water fountain. Squatting on their haunches with a dozen other people, their brows beaded with sweat, they waited restlessly for the all-clear signal.

This first bombardment sent Papa back to his childhood, reminding him of his experiences twenty-five years earlier with his mother.

When they finally left the damp and poorly reinforced basement, they were dazed by a cloud of dust rising from the other café, now demolished. How lucky they were to have chosen the right café for shelter. The Germans clearly were much closer than they had thought, as they were now randomly bombing targets, possibly to test the efficiency of the French Battery of Air Defense (DCA) before they went for bigger targets. At the time, they were starting off with only light bombs, the way a bonfire is set by a single match, but the damage when they enlarged their targets would be disastrous.

Splitting from his relatives and anxious about the truck, Papa spent the night at a small hotel, where he was awakened by an early phone call from his father-in-law. Louis Avot, for once, sounded particularly nervous. "Well, Émile, where are you? Have you seen the headlines?"

"Uh, but—" said Papa, still dazed from a bad night.

"Things are critical!" Bon Papa thundered. "I've decided to leave immediately for Douvrendelles. Do you have a car?"

"Yes, I do, but…" Papa realized that now his little truck would be carrying something a great deal more important than paper and prayed it would be ready. "Yes, I will come by as soon as I can."

"Fine," Bon Papa said. "I'm packing my suitcases." The line went dead. Papa was a bundle of nerves.

# 4

## RUNNING WITH FEAR

*P*apa raced downstairs to get a paper. Before he could even find the correct change, he read the huge headline from a block away: "*C'est La Guerre!*"

The Germans were crossing the Belgian border, heading into France.

His heart raced as he pictured his family home, a little dot on a map, just a finger's width away from the Belgian border from which all of hell's fury was coming. Momentarily disoriented, but all the more determined, he picked up the truck. At this time, new vehicles were equipped with a speed constraint, which held them down to a mere thirty-five miles per hour for the first hundred miles to break in the motor.

Exacerbating the situation was a large sign glued to the rear window that read *En Rodage* (Breaking In). This was designed to signal to the drivers behind it to be patient, but it also advertised that this was a new vehicle, not favorable given the current state of affairs.

"*Mais*, Monsieur," he said to the attendant, "don't you understand that I can't be driving this truck with this placard? It's like waving a red flag to anyone to steal it because it's new! Can't you just take it off?"

"Ah, *non*, Monsieur, that is impossible, that is against the rules, against the law," replied the Peugeot employee.

"But the war has been declared, we are in a state of emergency! I have to go to Paris, and then to Normandy, and then to the North! Please do it for me." My father tried to hand him some money.

"Monsieur, Monsieur! That would not be correct. It is not acceptable. I cannot help you at all. I am sorry, but the law is the law. We cannot remove the sign, and we cannot take off the restraint. You must take it to your mechanic to do that when you have passed the first hundred miles. I am deeply sorry."

Incredibly frustrated, somehow Papa made it to Paris by noon. He found Bon Papa irritated by the long wait.

"But, Émile, don't you realize how crucial it is that we get out?" he exclaimed.

"Yes, yes, I do, but Peugeot refused to take the restraint off the truck."

"Why didn't you pick it up last week?"

Bon Papa could be so illogical.

"I just couldn't." Papa tried not to be curt. "It wasn't ready."

"I'm surprised at you, Émile. You are usually so well organized." Anxiety laced the words of his father-in-law. "This is not the time to let us down. Elisabeth and the children can't be on their own."

Elisabeth, of his many children, was his favorite.

"No, no, I realize that. Let me concentrate on driving. We must get to Douvrendelles before nighttime. Thank God it is on the way home. I really have to get there tonight."

Then, in a silent panic growing with every mile, an iron band crunching his heart, he drove until late that afternoon, finally delivering his father-in-law and housemaid into safe hands at the Château de Douvrendelles and moving on.

It was well into the night when he reached Abbeville, still fifty-two miles from home. It was around this point that my normally so astute father realized that he was the only vehicle on the road. He was crossing through a completely deserted town when a man with a helmet popped out of a doorway and waved frantically to him. Terrified, Papa accelerated past him as fast as the truck would allow.

And this happened again and again. A little man would burst out of a doorway and attempt to get Papa to stop. In response, Papa would push the pedal down as hard as he could in his little "breaking-in" truck. He thought he heard, in spite of the humming of the motor, some dull sounds, but in his panicked state he was not sure of their direction or even their existence. It was only when he reentered the countryside and saw a huge sugar factory in flames that he realized the whole city was under attack. The bold men from the civilian defense had been trying in vain to flag him down to the safety of a reinforced basement.

"Murderers!" he yelled, shaking his fist. He lit a Gauloise between his quivering lips and drove on, his fear growing with every mile. "Darn this new truck," he thought, "I can't get out of *En Rodage* until I get it to my mechanic back home. What bad luck to be stuck at this idiotic speed when the roads are empty. I could get killed, and no one would find me under a bomb!"

It was the middle of the night when, exasperated, he finally made it home to Blendecques. Upon seeing the house unharmed, he felt a moment of relief before realizing that time was running out all over again. This was a pattern all of us became very familiar with very quickly: the lack of time. Everyone old enough to keep an eye open at that late hour was anxiously awaiting him. Bernard, Édith, and I were fast asleep.

Avoiding German troops parked in the backyard, Papa burst through the front door, dashing into the cellar to desperately embrace Maman. His eyes welled up with tears of relief, his whole body shaking from the exhaustion of driving 250 miles in the new truck under so much stress. Only the night before, he had escaped death sheltered in a café. Only the night before, small planes had been fighting above our heads while bullets peppered the sky, one of which crashed through our front door. Only the night before, Nazis had pounded on our front door, telling us to get out.

All those times before when we hid in the cellar in response to the blaring sirens, they were only warnings. They would sound from a distance, and we would respond. We would be scared, but then we would feel safe again. But no one can ever be completely prepared for the real thing. This time it was for real; our backyard had been invaded by the enemy. The bullet that pierced our house and our hearts, the "little bullet that could," turned us into refugees.

The next day we evacuated. Life as we knew it was now lost to all of us forever.

# 5

## ABANDONMENT

*T*he next day brought one more dawn, the last one that was left of my childhood. I was only four and a half years old.

The advancing German army was a terrifying dynamo, moving west and south much faster than predicted. They had poured in through Belgium, having run through the Ardennes, and crossed the River Meuse. With ease they had broken through severely weak French defenses down to the French border, only six miles from our house, and now we had them in our own backyard. Papa had known for days that we were vulnerable but was horrified by the sheer speed of the swarm of German soldiers to our doorstep.

Long before that fateful day, Papa had advised his business associates that if the Germans should invade Belgium, he would immediately leave Blendecques. He had been subjected to such terror in 1914 that no matter the condition of his business affairs, he would not risk exposing his children to the horrors of war. And now he was almost too late. Would he get us out of their invasion safely? Without a moment to lose, he was up before any of us and called Arthur for help.

As part of his preparations, he had commissioned a solid two-wheel trailer to be hitched to our new Matford automobile. By luck, the trailer had been delivered just a few days before the bullet had splintered the front door. Hitching was slow and difficult, for in spite of the need for haste, he wanted to be careful not to dent the fender of the priceless new car.

"Arthur, *faites attention*, be careful. We'll get it right."

Seeing Maman approach to watch them work, he pulled her aside. "Elisabeth," he said in a low voice, "I don't have to tell you how important it is that you drive most carefully."

"Of course I will," she nodded. Her hand fell softly on his arm. "I will be very careful."

"Remember, the extra weight of the gold will make the car more difficult to maneuver, especially in the turns and on the small roads."

"Yes, yes, I am aware of that. The precious cargo, the gold, the children. I will take care of them. I think I can do it." Her voice failed her; she broke into tears.

He tried to console her. "There's nothing you or I or *anyone* could have done, chérie," Papa said.

Maman looked up at him, her anguished face slightly relaxing, hoping for something positive.

"They call it *blitzkrieg*, their lightning war strategy; they come without warning, without mercy, en masse, in barrages. It's a shock attack, and we have no chance of surviving in this mayhem. We have to go *now*."

Maman's face turned calm and blank. Her pupils were dilating as Papa illustrated our dilemma.

"It's all over the papers in Paris. These German storm troopers at our door will become a terror, not just a stray bullet."

She nodded, sighed, slowly walked back toward the house, her feeling of dejection evident in the slump of her shoulders.

Papa stopped, blotting his glistening face with a handkerchief; he paced a few steps and lit a cigarette. Silence ensued as he inhaled, his eyes darting up and down in urgent calculation. Suddenly, he called to the servants. "Arthur, Léontine! We need to move fast! Make sure we have the food packed, and Mademoiselle, get all the children in the car. Make haste, please. We haven't much time."

In the growing activity there were so many details to consider; yet there was no doubt in his mind that to move his family south immediately was not soon enough. We had become a hot zone so suddenly that we had no time left to salvage more then a few armfuls of belongings. Papa's preparations were not as meticulous as he'd wanted, and he felt vulnerable scrambling at the last minute. In a matter of twenty-four hours we were leaving the house, our sanctuary, our hearth, our anchor, with only a few garments and as much food as we could carry.

The truck and trailer were filling up to the rafters with provisions; even we little ones helped to carry bags of food and a few garments hastily thrown in suitcases. We were all toting supplies to the truck like frenzied mice.

Sweet Fanny was lumbering in front of me, hauling a burlap bag of rice in her little arms. As she tried to lift the awkward package, she dropped it. Fanny had this propensity for dropping things. Whenever anything fell in the house, we would all call out "*Signé Fanny!*" no matter who dropped it. She looked down at the bag and back up to the truck, stymied about the next step, while we urged her to please pick it up and hand it over. I put the bag back in her arms like her dolly, and she was able to lift it properly.

My oldest sister, Charlotte, in a flippant attempt to relieve the gravity of our crisis, exclaimed in contrived excitement, "Hurrah, we're going on a trip!" But she quickly resigned herself to silence when she saw Maman crying. We heard Papa say to her, "Take a good look. This may be the last time we see it."

It was the first time that Maman bent over my shoulder and carefully pushed a pin through a tiny piece of paper. The pin made a loud pop as it pierced the flesh of the paper. Her hand was shaking at first, but then her tenacity and muscle memory took over. Maman continued with gentle ease as she attached my only form of identification to the thin cotton of my undershirt. The look on her face was so intense. She was not concerned that she would pinch me with the sharp metal as she softly whispered for me to hold still. No, her concern was much greater.

She had crafted these papers for fear we would get lost or separated. Maman had written our name, address, and destination for each of us to have safely secured to our clothing. This ceremonial pinning became a marker of our every move. Maman kept those papers in a little envelope throughout the war, adding one for each of us each time we moved, which was often.

We didn't have time for cloying good-byes; we were losing our roots, leaving our home. We scrambled into the vehicles and departed. We never saw any of it again.

# PART TWO

# 6

# AFFLUENCE AND PROSPERITY

BLENDECQUES - P.-de-C.          Le Château de Westhove

*The Château de Westhove was built by my great-grandfather, Prudent Avot, as he expanded his family to four sons and four daughters and an army of servants. Nicknamed the "White House," his neighbors quickly dubbed it the biggest error of the century.*

*M*aman's father, Louis Théophile Émile Avot, was the fourth of eight children born to my maternal great-grandparents, Prudent Auguste Joseph Avot and Justine Ursule Marie Maxellande Vallée. At the time, they were one of the wealthiest couples in the North of France.

Prudent Avot and his brother Émile arrived in Blendecques in 1870. The brothers, born exactly two years apart, looked like twins. Extremely tall and handsome, wearing small pointed beards in the style of Edward VII (called *à la impériale*), they had an imposing allure of refinement, especially when wearing their top hats. They wished to pursue careers in the paper business, and together purchased a small water mill operating as a cotton-weaving machine, which they transformed into a paper mill. Soon their differing conceptions of business, conflicting temperaments, and individualistic points of view clashed. After two years, Émile abandoned his older brother to build an identical competitive business just a few miles away, unfortunately destined to struggle and fail.

On his own, Prudent prospered as he enlarged, improved, renovated, and modernized his small paper mill. This was squeezed between a hill and a river, intersected by the main road and next to railroad tracks. His favorite saying was "*n'y allez pas, apportez le* (don't go there, bring it here)," so he pushed for a railway station to be built close to the mill and paid for its construction. To transport goods, he also built and paid for a canal from the river to the station. These improvements enhanced Prudent's reputation as a visionary. He became a famous self-made man who conceived and created a very successful paper business, manufacturing a wide variety of goods sold in France, Belgium, the Netherlands, Denmark, Sweden, and Germany.

With his growing fortune, Prudent built a village of small houses for the families of his factory workers, for which he was highly praised, and on a whim bought an entire hill of hundreds of acres of forests and fields, on which he built a mansion of grandiose proportions, *Le Château de Westhove*—also known as *La Maison Blanche* (the White House)—for which he was highly criticized.

Quickly dubbed *la plus grande erreur du siècle* (the biggest error of the century), the lavish home of my maternal grandparents, their four sons, and four daughters quickly became a symbol of the *haute bourgeoisie*, smacking of snobbism and pretension. The wealth of those Northern France industrialists at the end of the last century is mind-boggling, but they lived with middle-class ways and never mentioned money. Their only luxury, in a region known for its disagreeable climate of fogs and rains, was their home, seldom entered by strangers, and the accumulation of furniture, draperies, rugs, paintings, and bibelots filling the rooms.

Prudent's mansion galled and rankled nearly everyone. "How dare he, what nerve, it's preposterous," was on every tongue behind his back. Built of imported Italian bricks and stones, it was the mega-mansion of its day, with a gatehouse, a court entrance graced with a water pond crowned with a marble statue that spouted water from a Greek urn, a gravel driveway lined with poplars leading to a *porte-cochère* for horse and carriage, and several entrances consigned to specific services. Dormers, turrets, gables, and lunettes assured the neighbors that this was a personal badge of his solid one-upmanship and that he was lord of the mansion and cared nothing for his critics.

The interior of high ceilings and immense rooms, crowded with sumptuous antiques and imports of all kinds, demanded that their army of servants keep it in order. From the marble entrance to the mosaic floors and long vertical windows, you reached a ballroom of walls encrusted with mirrors in carved gold frames, interspersed with painted vines and climbing roses growing from the parquet floor to reach a pale blue sky dotted with white clouds and colorful birds, dominated by archangels enveloped in golden tulles playing little harps in the rounded corners. If given a rare invitation, you could visit the billiard room, several living rooms, a library, two studies, dining rooms, kitchen, storage, and so on. Notable was Prudent and Ursule's private chapel with a sacristy facing the little river from the second floor. Following strict Catholic dogma, the bedrooms directly above the chapel could never be used for guests.

Grandmother Ursule Maxellande, a beautiful woman happy in a cocoon of luxury, security, love, and children, traveled often with her husband to civilized countries like Austria and Italy, accompanied by her servants, who took care of her glamorous Poiret—fashion designer of the moment—wardrobe packed in Louis Vuitton luggage. Not for her Turkey or Morocco, where she detested the smells, the food, and the water, and the beggars, children, and animals underfoot, but where he reveled in collecting dubious artworks acclaimed as true archaeological treasures. Her days at home were spent in the *salon rose,* cozy in a magnificent rocking chair draped in an *aubergine*-colored damask, the north light window on her left, knitting little booties for the poor, making Irish lace at the speed of a sewing machine, or embroidering yet one more little pillow for another newborn.

After Mass each morning, before coming down the regal staircase, she decorated her ample bosom with an extraordinary brooch that would have made Elizabeth Taylor green with envy. The massive diamond with beveled edges was surrounded with marquise sparklers, each of which could easily have been an acceptable gem in an engagement ring for any of her four daughters.

Although the clip was extremely secure, the jeweler had added a sort of Hercules bar to fix it on her corsage, as well as a lovely gold chain ending in a safety pin studded with dots of rubies that added to its scintillating beauty.

In this monumental French country house, built about the same time as Frederick William Vanderbilt built Hyde Park on the Hudson River, the formal living-room furniture was always covered in white sheets, except when used, just once a year in May. This was on the occasion of the annual rite of Confirmation of the parish children, attended by *Monsigneur L'Évèque du Diocèse d'Arras.* Prudent's generous donations to rebuild and enlarge the church, install two hand-constructed organs, build new schools, and pay the staff, as well as building a new manse for the priest and a vicarage for the vicar, made him the host to this exceptional religious reception, the most important of the year, attended by hundreds from the parish of the *Departement du Pas-de-Calais*.

In 1913, Pope Pius X decorated Prudent Avot with the Pontifical Equestrian Order of St. Gregory the Great (Latin: *Ordo Sancti Gregorii Magni*, Italian: *Ordine di San Gregorio Magno*), one of the five Orders of Knighthood of the Holy See. This special honor was in recognition of his service to the Roman Catholic Church with his generous donations and bottomless beneficence. The talisman was a beautiful gold cross inset with precious stones, held on a wide red ribbon bordered in yellow, which he sported on many occasions. He had a mini-copy made for his wife and demanded she wear it to church every Sunday.

As they grew up and finished their studies, most of Prudent's sons and sons-in-law joined the firm, the Avot-Vallée paper industry, which still carries the same name today. Of all those relatives, his middle son, my grandfather Bon Papa Louis Avot, became the chief executive when Prudent retired. That is how Papa began his career in the paper business when he married Maman in 1926.

Prudent was an unstoppable workhorse who made fortunes with everything he touched. Back in 1825, a company called Verrerie des Sept Écluses, named for the seven locks on the River Aa, was established by Alexandre des Lyons de Noircam, who began to manufacture glass storage containers known as *dame-jeanne* (demijohns), which were popular at that time. In subsequent years, the company diversified into dining glassware, but by 1895 a lack of foresight and modernization was pushing it toward bankruptcy. As luck would have it, its buildings adjoined the paper mill, which Prudent was anxious to expand so he could produce cardboard. He bought the glass business, named it Verrerie Cristallerie d'Arques, and placed an ad for a manager in the local classifieds.

Georges Durand, twenty-seven, son of a glass engineer, was hired for the job. From 1897 onward, under Durand's competent managerial skills, the company prospered so much making glassware that in 1900

Prudent established a partnership called Avot-Durand, with four of his male heirs as partners, giving up the idea of having a cardboard factory on the site. To this day, the Durand family are the proprietors, and several of my cousins still work as executives in what is the world's leading manufacturer of crystal and glassware, under the brand names of Luminarc, Arcoroc, J. G. Durand, and Cristal d'Arques.

# 7

## $\mathscr{I}$ N S U L A T E D  $\mathscr{P}$ E A C E

$\mathscr{I}$t was January 1926, and Papa, not quite twenty-three, was thrilled to be pulled away from his own family's textile industry by a man he adored from the moment he met him: his father-in-law, Bon Papa Louis Avot. Papa was well aware of the status of his bride's great-grandfather, the venerable Prudent Avot, whose obituary in the papers had greatly impressed him when he was only fourteen years old. There was no reason Papa could not succeed with every endeavor he initiated. His brilliant studies and bottomless curiosity tagged him as gifted, smart, and diplomatic. He excelled at understanding every phase and level of a very complicated business, and this knowledge certainly became a godsend during the war years when he was Général de Gaulle's emissary on secret missions to Berlin.

When he joined Avot-Vallée Paper Industries in 1926, Papa was driven to succeed by Great-Grandfather Prudent Avot's lasting power and Grandfather Louis Avot's unfailing knowledge. He became part of the family associates, at least a dozen were on the payroll, learning every detail of the extensive paper-manufacturing business. Prodded ahead by his mentor, Papa had to be careful not to step on the toes of all the relatives working around him, some for quite a number of years. There was plenty of unprincipled backbiting, jealousy, and pernicious infighting, but he ignored it all, with his eyes on a possible leadership position.

There was a lot to learn, from the sources of incoming supplies to the destinations of outgoing products of the many specialized factories scattered in industrial cities throughout the North. These factories included recycling plants and plants that manufactured newspaper, thick brown wrapping paper, cardboard, business papers, and superfine watermarked linen-quality papers for private stationery. Even the extra-thin papers used for the famous Gauloises cigarettes, which first appeared in 1910, were made by Avot-Vallée; the winged helmet of the Greek goddess Victory still adorns those blue packages today.

Since he was flourishing financially and kept needing more space for his growing family and servants, Papa decided to negotiate for some land from Bon Papa Avot, who owned not only the paper mills but also acres of real estate in the region. He maintained the majestic 1850s Château de Douvrendelles and was considering an overhaul to make it habitable for our family. However, my parents strongly opposed this idea, seeing no end to the necessary renovations and, God forbid, becoming the resident welcome committee to the crowd of family showing up every Sunday for the weekly reunion and luncheon after ten o'clock High Mass. Instead, he convinced Bon Papa that building a new house to his own scale on some corner of the property would be more practical. After much cajoling from his favorite daughter, Bon Papa agreed. In 1928, on his own plot of four acres, Papa built a brand-new house within his budget and to his specifications. Only twelve years later, all his dreams were shattered by that bullet through the front door.

BLENDECQUES - P.-de.C. - Le Château Gaillet

*Papa built this lovely house in 1928 on a hilltop of four acres on the corner of Bon Papa's property. With central heating and running water, it was considered the most modern residence in the county.*

*It is summer 1935, and Maman is expecting me in this photo, in front of our house.*
*Charlotte and Fanny are on the right, Elisabeth is on the left, and Bernard is on her lap.*

*Papa is holding Bernard, Charlotte is in her bathing suit, Fanny and Elisabeth are in matching dresses in this photo taken in Ostende in the summer of 1935. I was born six months later, in December.*

# 8

## A DISAPPOINTING BIRTH

*The author at three years old in her black velvet hat and coat collar,*
*thick wool socks, and lace-up booties, circa 1938. I was the quietest child*
*in the family, not speaking until I was almost four years old.*

hen I came into this world, both Maman and I screaming in the middle of the night, a monster storm drummed thunder over our heads, and shards of lightning struck our rooftop. It was December 1, 1935, and our cries of pain were predicting the pandemonium that was to envelop my youth. I was destined to be a war child.

In 1940, I shared my fifth birthday with a devastating war and the loss of my safety. Thrown with my family into the chaos of the greatest war the world has ever known, I was never again to find security until I was ten, but by then I knew too much to ever experience a normal life. I had lost my youth.

There was a family battle that began long before my conception: keeping a son alive. My parents tried again and again, despite the heartbreak that must have accompanied the death of a set of premature twin boys and a seemingly healthy, full-term son, all lost in crib deaths. My only surviving brother, Bernard, was their first and last victory in this struggle. Fifteen months after him I was born, a dispiriting event of great proportions.

No matter how supportive she was of Papa's wish to have another son, I hope that Maman was ready to accept another daughter. At times I had to rattle the side of my crib to beg for my share of attention. Born strong and sturdy, healthy and serious, shuffled without undue vigilance among all the others, I was right from the start often *délaissée* (neglected), forsaken, an exceptionally quiet child. But as I grew, Maman affirmed her love for me in quiet, gentle ways: a small caress, a special treat, an unexpected compliment. She reassured me through life that she loved me deeply, as much as she did the others.

I was the fifth of six surviving children, but my three deceased brothers were never discounted. We had little embroidered numbers on many of our shirts, shorts, and scratchy wool bathing suits. Charlotte (November 1926) was 1; the twins Émile and Pierre (February 1928), and the next son Émile-Pierre (September 1929), all deceased, 2, 3, and 4 were held in their honor; Fanny (February 1932) was 5; Elisabeth (May

1933) 6: and Bernard (September 1934) was 7. I (December 1935) was 8, and the baby, Édith, (May 1938) was 9. The coming of the war was the final blow for childbirth.

Maman was, for the first time, nervous about giving birth, terrified in fact. Whenever she recalled my arrival, she would say how much she apprehended my coming, blaming this anxiety on the commotion of the storm. Or was it that she couldn't stand the idea of another girl? It had never happened with her other babies. She wondered if her unusual fear and the storm were omens for the life she was about to give birth to. That big storm, harrowing Maman so deeply, was a message of prophetic significance. By the tender age of ten, half of my life had been spent in safe family surroundings, and half had been shattered by a war that nearly destroyed us all.

For weeks I remained nameless. One day the name Hélène popped up for no reason. Maman regretted many times she did not call me by her grandmother's name, Maxellande, a single name sufficient to obliterate all the ones I do have now: Hélène Thérèse Anne Cornélie Gaillet de Barcza de Neergaard. I can't begin to think how I would have coped with the nickname Max.

My parents came from devout Catholic families, a faith that certainly contributed to their starting their own family overnight. They were married in January 1926, and their first child, Charlotte, arrived in November of that same year. By the time I arrived, my parents were only thirty-one years old. Altogether, Maman was pregnant seventeen times, had nine children (one set of twins), and nine miscarriages, including three during the war. More than once, she nearly died in childbirth. I remember how often we'd find her exhausted in a *chaise longue* or on her bed, begging us to be quiet.

With unqualified blessings, this marriage was solid from its very beginning, thanks to my grandfather, Bon Papa Louis Avot, who took my father under his wing the day he gave away his daughter, Elisabeth, the fourth of his eight children, to Émile Pierre Gaillet, who was himself the fourth of five.

BLENDECQUES. — Château du Hamel.

*The Château du Hamel belonged to my grandfather, Bon Papa Louis Avot; it is where Maman was born. She was one of eight children, four boys and four girls, all of whom had many children themselves.*

# 9

## RESOURCEFUL DOMESTICITY

We lived in the little village of Blendecques, between Lille and Calais in the North of France, only six miles from the Belgian border. Large Catholic families populated this region, and though it was not a race as to which family would have the most children in the shortest time possible, we were, nevertheless, known all over the country as *Les Grandes Familles du Nord* (the large families of the North). Between my parents and their siblings, there were ninety-eight first cousins.

Two little girls were born to close relatives the same week I was: one to Papa's younger sister, Tante Thérèse, who became my godmother, and the other to one of Maman's brothers, Oncle Etienne, which automatically made him my godfather, a lucky draw, since he was Maman's favorite brother. We became very close over the years.

Always avant-garde in his calculations, installing the latest amenities, Papa made his new house as modern as possible. I remember it as warm and comfortable. Once I get past the sharp pang of loss, the trip down memory lane takes me to a little hill with a lovely view south, down a slope to the River Aa. To the north, I recall a dark-red protective brick wall with large round holes along the top that separated us from the country road. To the east, where we would watch the sunrise, an ancient paper mill appeared on the horizon, its white smoke fluttering from tall brick stacks. Beyond the mill, the sky would go ablaze with the dawning radiance of the sun. Every sunrise was so special, I could see it from my window while saying my prayers if awakened early enough.

This home was warm because it had central heating when so many of our relatives' places had no heat at all. And it was warm because it was the last safe place of my childhood. Its palatial walls echoed our joy and laughter so loudly they seem to trickle on for eternity. If I were to appear there today by some means of fantasy, I would expect to still hear the faint reverberation of our little voices, laughing. The joy is so unbroken; it is just beyond tangible even now.

I can feel the heat from the bottom of my patent leather shoes as they slid across the slick marble floor of the grand entrance hall, racing past my sister Fanny as she strolled back and forth with her dolly in a pale-blue pram. I remember dodging Elisabeth's bouncing ball as I landed hard into the front door that seemed to be repeated in miniature in the windows and the arcade doors that separated our version of a perfect world from dangers outside.

I remember my brother being reprimanded and sent to the garden for running his bright-red pedal car in the hall, and the giggling of us girls as we watched his face flush with a childlike combination of embarrassment and anger as he respectfully obeyed orders. With one final defiant turn toward us, he would raise his eyebrows, his look mischievous once more, as if to say, "I don't mind, I like it outside. There's much more trouble out there."

*Bernard and Maman out for a walk on the esplanade of the beach
in Ostende where my parents often went for weekends. Note how well
dressed they both are, down to the white gloves in her hand.*

Whatever the source of that warmth that still tickles my cheeks like the first cracks of a bonfire, when I think back on it, I doubt that it was the central heating or the woodburning fireplaces that laced several beautiful rooms with their enchanting glow on winter nights. Safety is what it was, safety and the all-encompassing love we had for each other.

The lighting was modern and ambient. Every nook and cranny that might need to be seen had its own light source, which made hiding games at home that much more of a challenge. I didn't know that not all children had built-in bookcases in their rooms. But we all did. I was very unaware of the well-stocked, full-size basement being more than a fact of life—it was a little piece of my world that was just there. Even when the sirens would blare, and we would retreat into this comfortable version of a basement, things were still mostly matter-of-fact, and my innocence was still intact.

Our parents were as strict as was necessary for a family of our size. They didn't see us much during the day. Papa left for work early and returned only for dinner. When Bon Papa Avot decided to retire and move to Paris in 1938, running the paper business absorbed Papa completely. The factories were showing signs of disrepair and neglect in several sectors. The sales department was weak and desperately needed new blood and refurbishing. The competition was becoming fierce, with new machines and modernized techniques, and a nascent international market demanded special skills. Thus, Papa's responsibilities were greatly increased and diversified. Monthly trips to Paris for meetings with syndicates and associations added to the number of his disappearances and inability to make preparations for the upcoming crisis.

Maman was kept busy around the property with household duties, visiting relatives in the nearby countryside or going into Lille to shop. She never had to stray too far from her homeland. Maman had gone from being a daughter in a large family to being the mother of many children, and the voyage had covered only a few miles. We were a shining example of *Les Grandes Familles du Nord*. Even if only three families got together, the dining-room table would be set for at least twenty-four, with a couple dozen children running around. Always dressed up for church on Sundays, we had to be careful not to stain or tear our dresses playing games outdoors, climbing trees, running, hiding in outbuildings, and inventing all sorts of group games, as we had few toys at that time.

Sunday was the only day of the week we wore our specially handmade clothes, not hand-me-downs. Each of the girls had her special dress and shoes, white cotton panties, a hand-knit sweater with her number on it, and a little coat, all matching. The rest of the week, we wore what didn't fit our older sister, from Charlotte to Fanny to Zabeth to Hélène to Édith. My brother had three outfits, one for Sundays and two for weekdays, alternating them from day to day.

When she would travel, Maman would leave us in the capable hands of our loyal attendants. Our live-in governess, whose room was on the third floor and completely off-limits to us children, was a woman of care and wisdom. She kept us well behaved without ever uttering a loud word or showing the slightest hint of frustration. We had a butler, Arthur, who doubled as our chauffeur if Maman wanted to go to town. His wife, Léontine, was our cook, and she never strayed far from the kitchen. Her domain went from kitchen to garden to dining room and to her quarters, rarely beyond. They had come from my grandmother's house and lived with us in separate servants' quarters beyond the kitchen.

Other help—the seamstress, gardeners, caterers, housemaids— would come on a daily basis, often working for other relatives as well. Many of those who worked for us stayed on with Avot families for years. Many returned to their families at the break of the war and came back after the Liberation. As for Arthur and Léontine, they stayed on bravely through all our adventures, leaving only when they were well into their eighties to go home again to be with members of their family they hadn't seen in years. Truly, we considered them to be our own family and admired them as saints.

*During our youth, we were never spoiled with candy, ice cream, toys, or clothes. The war ended the occasional rare treats for all of us. L–R: Charlotte, Fanny, Elisabeth, Hélène, and Bernard, circa 1938–39.*

# PART THREE

# 10

## EVACUATION

The Nazis had shattered our door with a bullet and slammed their guns into it, throwing us into a state of panic. The next day we were gone, abandoning everything we'd ever known.

Officers and their rank and file soon realized ours was the most comfortable residence in the area and established their headquarters in it. My parents were relieved by this stroke of luck, praying their presence would protect our house from bombardments and annihilation.

With wine in the cellar, loads of food in the pantry, linens for every bedroom, and real toilet paper in each bathroom, these usurpers made themselves at home. Unwilling peasants and factory workers were forced to work for them from early in the mornings until late at night, returning home exhausted and disgusted by their labors. Cleaning, cooking, washing up, laundry, ironing, and a multitude of daily tasks were forced on them, and they endured a language barrier that made it all the more unbearable. The officers in charge were polite and distant, obviously a great deal more comfortable than if they had settled in old farmhouses or forbidding châteaux. With all our furniture and personal belongings at their disposal, they stayed there throughout the four years of their occupation of France.

Papa heard rumors that the officers took turns desecrating his and Maman's bedroom by bringing in French whores from nearby towns who plied their trade among the troops. Few of these women survived.

After the Liberation, they were arrested, had their heads shaved, were paraded in the streets, insulted and spat on by their neighbors, and then executed on the spot by the French Resistance.

Meanwhile, we traveled with almost nothing. Each of us had the clothes on our backs and a tiny cardboard case with a couple more items, nothing that would last more than the summer. Mute desolation seeped from the walls of our village as we departed. Papa drove the Peugeot truck, weaving under the weight of its cargo, with Arthur ensconced in the middle of the seat, and Léontine holding on tight to my puny little brother on her lap. Older, but smaller than I was, Bernard wasn't growing well or strong, another deep worry for my parents. He coughed and slept a lot. I stayed close to protect him.

Making sure we were all in, expecting the worst, hauling the loaded trailer hitched behind, Maman grasped the wheel of our brand-new Matford as if it were the Holy Cross in a procession to Calvary and followed Papa blindly. The baby was strapped on Maman's lap with an elastic belt around their waists. Our governess, on the right front seat, had her lap and surroundings full of baby gear and food bags. The four older girls, prone to attacks of motion sickness, were piled up in the back. We always sat in the same seats: Fanny and Zabeth in the middle and Charlotte on the left. I was always in the right backseat, still to this day the only seat I feel safe in if I am not driving.

When you are a child, you don't have to understand a catastrophe to feel the depth and hurt of it. By the time the mind is able to comprehend what happened, wounds are deeply embedded in the soul. Terrified, I cringed at my window, a sliver of air helping to control the queasy feeling rising up in my throat, making me ill and dizzy. To counteract the rocking of the car, I pushed my hip against the door, restlessly watching the road over Nanny's shoulder, holding my breath for fear of nausea and the possibility that even my breathing could be a nuisance. We didn't talk in the backseat; we didn't even look at each other. No words could alleviate our distress.

Somewhere along the way, Papa was stopped for lack of a registration plate on the trailer and got a traffic ticket that he promptly lost and forgot. On this barren road, abandoning our village, losing everything he had built up, heartbroken and fearful of what was ahead, he was somehow able to focus on what had to be done. He had a destination, and he aimed to reach it. Carefully, he chose smaller country roads going southwest in the direction of Bon Papa Avot's Château de Douvrendelles in the Departement de la Haute Normandie.

The world as we knew it was gone. And with it, our childhood.

*Our family got together every Sunday after High Mass at my grandfather's château. Bon Papa is in the center, right. To his right is Bonne Maman, and directly in front of her is the author, looking up at the sky. On my left is my brother, Bernard. Maman is in the center top row looking sideways, my godfather, Oncle Etienne, one of her brothers, is half-hidden back on the right, very tall. In front of him with the V-neck dress is their youngest sister, Tante Jacqueline. Photo taken in 1937.*

# 11

## SHELTER IN A CHÂTEAU

*P*apa drove slowly on dusty, forlorn roads, annoyed by the ticket for lack of a trailer registration. "So stupid," he thought. "What will they think of next? Why don't they help those poor people who don't know where to go? Why don't they organize this evacuation? Why? Why? WHY?" He was so frustrated by his own incompetence.

He tried to push the new truck to a better speed but was dragged down by the heavily laden Matford in its wake with family, gold treasure, and trailer. Weary, he stopped for lunch to grab a bowl of soup with a thick slice of peasant bread and a couple more times for bouts of nausea or relief behind bushes. Alerted by honking from the Matford, they filled up with gasoline at a small village station. With all of these stops, the 113-mile trip from Blendecques to Douvrendelles took eight tedious hours. We arrived after sunset, deeply fatigued. My grandfather, ragged with anxiety, was extremely relieved to see us.

In spite of having escaped our warring home front, none of us felt safe, as we had covered only a meager distance. Papa was well aware of our daunting situation. If the Germans were to push their attacks in our direction, there wouldn't be much time for family reunions. He knew the Germans were advancing on the important seaport of Dunkirk and dreaded the kind of massacre that might take place there.

I remember being afraid. Not of the Germans, per se, as I suspect Papa was. I was concerned with what all small children are: Papa's discontent. There were moments when I was convinced he was going to pull his hair out as he ran his ink-stained fingers through it in distress. At times it was clear that he was a wreck. But every time he pursed his lips around a cigarette and dragged intently, it felt as if he were inhaling our tension, blowing out blue halos of smoke that rebounded upon his serene poise, contrived or not. His very presence filled me with fear, and I tried my best to make myself invisible. Still, my little girl's voice often filled the air with soft sobs.

To our relief, the staff of the château had prepared some food. It was such a gift to have a hot meal waiting in a huge dwelling with no running water or electricity. We ate dinner quickly and in silence. Despite our full bellies and the knowledge that we were extremely lucky to be together, it was a gloomy supper.

Papa ushered us off to bed in the same manner that he always did: "*Bonsoir, petite,*" with a slight smile. Maman gently took our heads between her hands, kissed each of our foreheads, marking it with the sign of the cross with her thumb, checked our shirts for the little paper tag, and we were off to bed without a whisper. Warm spring air made it unnecessary to light fireplaces or use extra blankets. Sleep helped us overcome our fears.

Bon Papa's retreat had many beds and, perhaps for the last time ever, we slept like babies.

# 12

## SOMBER UNCERTAINTY

We later learned that friends had labeled us cowards for being the first to leave our native village, not knowing how we'd been forced out. But when we ran into them after their harried migrations from the North of France, they conceded that Papa was probably lucky to have left immediately, as if a forced flight were a lucky draw. They described the formation of a massive exodus during which half the population from the North drifted to the South under debilitating circumstances.

Roads were clogged bumper to bumper with an array of vehicles rattling in the center and crowds of people dawdling on both sides, all heading south. Families were often forced to abandon their vehicles to escape the haphazard gunfire from low-flying German Stukas indiscriminately shelling these interminable convoys. Cars, trucks, buses, horses, bikes, even wheelbarrows crawled along with no place to go, no place to hide. There were fisticuffs and physical attacks at river crossings where antiquated barges still took you across the water for lack of bridges. With the savage onslaught of this war barely begun, they saw pets tossed out of vehicles as excess baggage. They saw children screaming for lost parents, adolescents trampled by throngs of strangers, housewives desperate to find their husbands, their babies. They saw dead bodies abandoned by the roadside, frozen in rigor mortis, sniffed by mongrels, circled by crows.

Looting was prevalent, committed by otherwise respectable people who had no other means of obtaining food. Refugees would filch anything they could grab as they meandered through deserted towns. Farmers would hide and, without hesitation, shoot the looters who strayed onto their farms. The news was bleak, the future a somber uncertainty.

My grandfather didn't have the same fears as Papa. He felt secure and had settled in for the duration in his staunch château. He had been elated to see us all arrive to keep him company, treating the situation as he would a family vacation. As each of Maman's sisters arrived with their large families in tow, Bon Papa would seem more and more jolly, while the pressure on our family was tangible.

Not only had we arrived first, but also we were the only family to have staff; all the others had returned to their families. Even worse, Papa was the only one who had thought to pack a large amount of provisions. More mouths to feed arrived, but they brought no additional food with them. Maman was in despair.

After hearing one of her sisters reprimanding Arthur for not making her bed, Maman simply would not stand for all the weight of the immense surge of people seeking shelter to fall on the shoulders of our beloved Arthur and Léontine. She would behave as a commander, not allowing her family to treat them badly. She talked to Papa about what she overheard, and that was the last that anyone spoke out of turn to our help. We all began to make our own beds and clear our plates, small chores alleviating the boredom.

Bon Papa was overjoyed to see my aunt's family, the Duponts from Cysoing, with their eight children. Then my other aunt's family, the Dansettes from Armentières, appeared with their seven children in tow, their staff gone. As Douvrendelles was such an immense domain, we all squeezed in to accommodate new residents. The situation seemed cozy with two or three children per bed, several beds per room. But the burden of work fell on the shoulders of my grandfather's staff of three and our faithful Arthur and Léontine, who never complained, even though you could see they were exhausted from the overload of work. Within days, the demands for food became difficult to fulfill.

Maman was distraught and foiled as more cars arrived with more relatives debarking with no provisions whatsoever. She begged Papa to check the supplies that were disappearing to prepare huge meals for everybody. We had to eat in shifts as the dining room table could accommodate only twenty-four at a time. All grown-ups first, then all the kids, some at small card tables. She rationed the food strictly to minimize waste and took it upon herself to zealously organize as best she could, to maintain the peace. Maman checked over and over, every night, to make sure all candles and kerosene lamps were extinguished. Her fear of fire was elevated by the lack of running water.

From the joyous first days of seeing that each family was safe, the mood in the château turned depressing. News reached us sporadically through hourly radio newscasts. All the adults would gather around the one radio located in a small library off the living room. Extra chairs had been brought in and surrounded the antique round table on which the old-fashioned radio sat about a foot high. An extension cord snaked along the carpet, inviting warnings to those walking around trying to get nearer to the unit.

Chatter became silence as the radio was turned on to warm up. It burped several times. It crackled static. It wheezed when slightly off station. Finally it spewed dire news from commentators droning in deep funereal voices. Hour after hour the news got worse, and the adults sighed in despair. "What are we to do?" they would whisper. "Where are we going to go? What do you think?" No one had answers.

Desolation encircled us children. Nothing was the same as before, and we were beleaguered by the chaos of war nearby, living in silence and apprehension. We could see the distress in our parents' faces, in their unusual reactions toward us: pushing us away, distant, or looking at us with tear-streaked faces. We had clear instructions about the protocol and knew what was expected of us. Do not talk during mealtimes. Do not put your elbows on the table. Do not kick a cousin under the tablecloth. Never start eating before the adults, and never clear your plate until everyone was finished. Our excitement at being with our cousins was destroyed by current events. Our joyfulness vanished.

This was the last of the big family reunions. We were never again reunited with all our cousins. Many we never saw again, despite their surviving the war. It was good-bye, but we didn't know it. Something dark and evil was claiming our world. What we felt then we could not have described, it was so deep and dark a power of helplessness.

Although we pretended to be OK, the sullen atmosphere impregnated all the children regardless of age. We weren't allowed outside for fear of snipers. We were quiet and forlorn. We lost our appetites, our laughter, and our youth. In the bedrooms we didn't scrap for bed space; we curled up and slept. We obeyed Mademoiselle, who helped us get dressed. We wore the same thing every day. Bags remained packed in the corners of every room, ready to go at a moment's notice.

# 13
## SAFETY NIGHTMARE

The Germans decided to attack by coming through Belgium. The speed of their attack, combined with the mobility of their Panzers and the support of their Stukas—dive-bombers that dropped twelve thousand parachutists—caught the French unprepared and defenseless. The first three French army divisions ran out of gasoline and could not hold back the tanks pushing through Charleroi, Belgium. The front at Sedan on the River La Meuse, ten miles from the Belgian border, caved in, creating a sweeping movement of panic among French troops. The town of Sedan was obliterated overnight. The French general leading a mission to hold them back was captured with his troops, and all survivors were made prisoners after burying their dead on the spot. Then the Germans, instead of heading south, unexpectedly veered to the west toward Calais, just barely north of us. Where we were, near the seaport of Dieppe just north of Normandy, was the next target in the line of fire.

We stayed only two weeks at Bon Papa's château. On May 20, the Germans flanked the port of Dunkirk. Papa's intuition was impeccable as far as knowing what to do, but before we could depart, he had to make some frantic calls to find our next refuge. This time we would be leaving without any provisions. Our sojourn at the château ended sooner than we anticipated, and the misery of the road was to envelop us once more.

As we waited for an assured destination, different branches of the family began to scatter like a flight of sparrows before a thunderstorm. Some went to Arcachon near Bordeaux, some to Nice, St. Tropez, and Biarritz on the Côte d'Azur. Others went directly down to Marseille, where they could find shelter with Papa's oldest brother, who owned a confectionery factory making black licorice that all of us hated and called *bonbons goudron* (tar candy). Before long the news announced that the Germans had reached the River Somme, only thirty-one miles north, tearing away our safety net.

Another of Papa's brothers had been living in Deauville, Normandy, for a while. The possibility of going there illumined Papa's horizons considerably. Even though it was only one hundred miles west of Douvrendelles, it had the enormous advantage of being southwest of the River Seine, which was very wide at that junction and deemed capable of holding back the enemy. At this time, gasoline was still readily available without coupons, so Papa had no difficulty going back and forth, helping the other families get to their destinations before the massive exodus from the north made it impossible to move on the roads.

Now it was time for Papa to move his own family, and he decided on Deauville. He reached his brother Oncle Robert and his wife, Tante Germaine. He tasked them with the errand of finding a rental large enough to accommodate Bon Papa, his personal maid, and us. Bon Papa had insisted on accompanying us, finally exhausted from more than twenty-five little grandchildren running underfoot, and fearful of a future alone. He had plopped himself heavily into one of the Windsor chairs in the main sitting room and burst out, "I will come, too. I need a vacation as much as any of you."

Tante Germaine didn't have to look very far to find us a villa; there was only one left for rent in the entire area. It was lovely, right on the beach in Trouville, a smaller destination next to Deauville. The owner demanded an exorbitant advance cash payment for a one-year lease, and with no other choice, Papa accepted. The night that this was finalized was a happy one.

Papa led us in prayer. We all knelt and said many Pater Nosters and Ave Marias for our indebtedness to the Lord for allowing us the good fortune to have been able to meet the demands of a greedy landlord. We were never allowed to forget that it was God who had given us these luxuries, and should we ever be found undeserving or ungrateful, He could take everything away.

We moved our pathetic caravan a hundred miles westward with Bon Papa in the lead, accompanied by two servants, my parents with their six children and three servants dragging behind. When we left, we acquired three more women, my grandmother, great-grandmother, and their attendant, who squeezed into the vehicles. Seventeen of us arrived at a small quiet seaside resort, facing the beginning of the worst war in history.

# 14

## SEASHORE AND SADNESS

*I*t was the end of May 1940. We were blessed to have secured that rental at the resort of Trouville-sur-Mer, east of Normandy, directly south across the harbor of Le Havre, on the coast of La Manche. We were in a little beachfront rental known as the Villa Neptune. As it was too small for all seventeen of us, Uncle Robert took in the grandmothers, and we kept the grandfather.

Along the wide coastline and pristine beach there was a very long nineteenth-century boardwalk similar to Coney Island's today. Our rental was right by the boardwalk and faced west onto the beach and the water. Behind us, lovely green hills were dotted with Second Empire mansions mixed with loads of smaller resort homes. Right around the bend on the River Touques was a large fishing port, Deauville, used by Parisians as an exclusive playground, with its own racetrack and casino. It all seemed so safe and out of the way that within hours, we felt liberated from our recent suffocating confinements.

My grandfather was the one to feel the squeeze of space most, but he refused to complain. At Maman's insistence that he should take the largest bedroom he exclaimed, "I can be comfortable anywhere, just give me a bed and a desk and a chair, and I'm happy!"

"But Papa," she insisted, "I can put more children in one room, they won't mind, they'll be outside all day."

"Absolutely not," he said. "You know my tastes are simple, Elisabeth. My father taught me that adaptation in any surroundings alleviates headaches and lumbago." And he settled on the smallest room, one in back away from the commotions of family activities and right next to his maid's room.

We giggled at that word, *lum-ba-go*, it sounded like a horrible disease. He had to explain it to us and added, "And I am just as happy to share the bathroom with everyone, it will teach you children to flush the toilet at all times!" Our education was certainly off to a jump start with Bon Papa around!

In May the seawater was much too cold to go swimming. Only the hardy types and boasters would venture into the water above a dip of their ankles. But swimming or no swimming, we were lucky, and we knew it. We finally got to stay outdoors without constant fear for our lives. We started to play again, making sand castles, marching to the tide going in and out on the very flat long sandy beach. We could squash the wet sand between our toes and etch big designs before the rising water flooded them. We discovered the pungent smell of the muddied sand at low tide, a smell that would follow us back to the house, even into our beds, three each in two bedrooms, and the parents in the last one.

We dug with our fingers to find the little crabs as they emitted air bubbles onto the surface, and we screamed when we found one still hidden in its shell trying to escape. Bernard and I would run to Maman, who was resting on a *chaise longue*. This beach is where we became as close as twins, always doing everything together. I was very protective of him from his three older sisters, who thought he was a moron. But he was only shy and weak and afraid.

"Maman, Maman, look! We have a little crab, he is in there, you can't see him but we know he is there!"

She would smile and sigh, always tired, despondent. But she'd pay attention and ask us to put him on the sand. "You'll see," she'd say, "after a moment he will come out and run to the sea." And she was right. How did she know that crab would strut off sideways? She knew everything, but didn't talk much. Mostly she was tired, and most likely in a quiet panic about our future.

We loved gathering dozens of seashells and stuffing them into our pockets and, like a funny cartoon, Mademoiselle would reach into our pockets as we lined up to come inside and throw everything back out onto the sand at our doorstep before letting us into the house for the evening. We were burying the hardships of our frightful escape, enjoying the discoveries such a great beach had to offer. Our lives were blithe and unencumbered at Villa Neptune, and we were lucky for those sacred days.

Life was very simple, down to just basics. Every day we wore the same thing. Scratchy hand-knit matching navy wool one-piece bathing suits with a white number knitted in on the chest, denoting which child we were. This we could cover up with navy-blue pull-on cotton shorts with an elastic waistband and two little pockets that we crammed with all sorts of seaside rubble.

For warmth we each had our treasure, a *pull marin*. This is a sailor's jersey. Think Rock Hudson basking in the cool sun in the 1957 film *A Farewell to Arms*, when he and Jennifer Jones first reach Switzerland. That is what our striped shirts were like. Originally designed with bright white stripes to locate a drowning sailor, ours were used to locate our cluster in a sea of people if trouble should come our way. We had no need for fashion and were all dressed alike. Given our discipline growing up and our current predicament, we always stayed close together. Other mothers on the beach would point to us and say, "Oh, my, look at all those poor little children." We probably looked more like a gang of orphans than the tourists we were trying to ape.

On rainy days we stayed indoors, playing games we invented, often grouped on the living room floor because Maman was exhausted and needed to rest in the afternoon. Bon Papa took long naps after his morning walk on the boardwalk, where he would bow to many passersby who recognized him as the patriarch of a large family.

Early mornings and late afternoons, the boardwalk was crammed with people walking the length of it and back again. It was a daily social ritual, an activity to see everyone you knew and hear all the gossip of the town. For us little ones, our short stay in Trouville was a time of delights, fresh food, deep sleep, physical activities, freedom from constraints, and probably a storage of good health for future ordeals that would not be so picturesque.

Meanwhile, my parents were sick with alarm, listening to the daily news pouring out stories about the war. Newspapers were becoming more difficult to find each morning. Neighbors would share one copy during the day, the original buyer always wanting his copy back. Newspapers were never thrown away, as they were used in many wily and ingenious ways. Fishermen used them to wrap fish at the market, housewives used them to clean the fish on their kitchen counter and wrap up the scraps so they wouldn't putrefy the garbage pail. We cut them up into smaller squares for toilet paper that we would hang on a twisted hook by the toilet. We would spread pages by the door where we left our sandals and wiped the sand off our feet. We stuffed them into the grown-ups' shoes to help keep their shape, wrinkled them up to wipe the salt off the windows, and, naturally, made paper hats, boats, chains, and dolls to play with since we had no toys.

Bon Papa would smile and make jokes with Arthur. "What did I tell you, old boy? Paper is a marvelous, much-needed thing!"

Laughing himself into a fit, his face would crease up into a ball of old skin. He would appear to be jolly and full of pride, boasting of all the usefulness of his paper. I think Arthur truly loved Bon Papa. He would laugh at other times, but I never saw him laugh as much as when Bon Papa got him going. The two of them would go on and on with their commentary on how wonderful paper was.

"Grand indeed," Arthur would retort. "Why, without paper, we would have to get the children actual toys."

This was an old game the two of them had come up with before I was born. Reportedly, Arthur had interviewed for his position and had made some faux pas regarding working for a man who ran a paper company.

"Well, without paper we would have nothing to wipe our..." As he stumbled trying to fill in the blank, he and Papa burst into laughter and were friends ever since.

The story had been told and retold to Bon Papa, and the two of them had kept this little game going ever since. I think Bon Papa was particularly pleased to have so many great examples about how wonderful and important paper was.

I think Papa refrained from this game because the feeling was all too familiar. He knew that the tempest would bring with it a scarcity of resources. With every reused or recycled newspaper page, a chill crawled deeper into his bones. He knew that something was on the horizon. He tried to smile as the horror grew, but it was no laughing matter.

# PART FOUR

# 15

## THE TEMPEST

The Germans invaded France with ferocious armored assaults that terrified civilians, who fled by the thousands. They advanced through Belgium destroying the main French defenses, fearless of reprisals. They continued without relent until May 24, when they swept into Dunkirk and trapped 330,000 French and British soldiers on the beaches. This onslaught could have been a deadly coup de grâce, but Churchill hollered, "We shall never surrender!" and rallied his troops with confidence.

Through a miracle of engineering warfare by the British Expeditionary Force, most of these soldiers were evacuated across the English Channel. Called Operation Dynamo, the rescue of thousands of troops from narrow beaches, a few men at a time on dozens of little boats, then transferred to larger ships offshore, went on day and night without letup until all of them escaped from Dunkirk. It was one of the finest hours for the British troops, a miraculous deliverance.

Papa listened with a heavy heart to news of this war raging on only 205 miles from us. He wept for the French struggling to escape the German troops. Barely settled in, my parents couldn't find it in their hearts to move us again or find the strength to make new plans to go, or consider where to escape to. So for the time being, we stayed.

We were only beginning to experience the torments that would continue to multiply by the day. This was June 1, 1940. We had been in our cozy home in Blendecques only three weeks before. We had traveled 213 miles and were no safer than on day one. In spite of the cost involved in this latest rental, Papa, armed with tenacity and resolve, came to the decision that we had to get away as far south as we could, to the smallest village that we could find, and as quickly as possible.

Papa had access to people and places because of his business ventures and his natural *savoir-faire,* which would serve him well in finding solutions. He located an associate who lived in a seashore village in southwest France whom he called for help.

"Allo, may I please speak with Monsieur Léon Monnet?"

"Oui, Monsieur, may I tell him who is calling?" answered a servant.

"Émile Gaillet, from Avot-Vallée…and it is urgent!" he added, wanting to skip all the niceties that a telephone call demanded.

"Allo, Émile, *ici* Léon, how are you? And the family?" His voice was smooth, agreeable, calming.

Papa asked all the right questions impatiently and lurched into his explanation of distress. "I hate to bother you like this, Léon, but the truth is that life here has become frightful, and I fear for all of us," he finally said.

Léon Monnet assured Papa that, should we decide to travel that far south, he would secure a place for us to live.

Still in Trouville, roaring motors awakened us one night and a series of explosions made us jump to the windows. Le Havre, the second most important seaport of France, just nine miles across the estuary of the Seine north of us, was on fire. The Germans in their terrifying Stukas were ruthlessly bombarding the city, regrouping above our heads to make another attack. The riotous din of the planes and volleys across the water shook the house to the rafters. The smell of smoke from the hypnotizing fires across the horizon wafted into our open windows. This smell clung to me, stayed on my skin, went into my clothes; now it lingers forever in my memory. To this day I am terrified of fire. That fear and the smell can never be erased. Unlike our doodles in the sand, no tide could ever wash that smell from me.

The scene was spectacular and macabre. Enemy salvos spared nothing—churches, schools, public and commercial buildings, industries—all were destroyed. It was entrancing and grotesque to watch as water mains were crushed, denying any possibility of putting out the fires, streets exploded into fragments, buildings crashed, and cars burned. Le Havre had nothing left standing; the city was pulverized. Over five thousand civilians were killed; over eighty thousand became homeless. Adding to the chaos already cramming the roads from Dunkirk were terrified civilians rushing south to escape, leaving behind everything they had ever known. Many never returned, forever refugees.

The silence that followed buried our hopes. Papa sent a cable to Monnet: "There are twelve of us coming." And once more, armed with more hope than knowledge, we got ready to move.

There's a French word that is hard to translate: *déguerpir*—meaning to clear off, scuttle away, skedaddle, scram—and that's exactly what we did, crammed into the vehicles, with almost no provisions but with renewed hope. Papa said we had already leaped over the two big rivers of the Somme and the Seine; there was no reason to think we couldn't jump now over the Loire and the Garonne.

Droves of refugees and French soldiers in retreat clotted all southern roads, so Papa mapped out an itinerary of secondary small routes, closely following the Atlantic coast. Armed with unflagging optimism and a daring wife who was also an excellent navigator, we continued our flight toward the South. We had a stack of Michelin maps, which fascinated me. Designs, colors, shapes, and lines let you follow your route from one town to the next and find your destination. I loved the feel and the smell of the paper, the system of refolding it correctly so you could see the thick name of Michelin in dark blue type on the cover, with a yellow border encircling a small version of the map printed inside.

"Never turn the map upside down," Maman would tell me. "Always keep your fingertip on where you are and stay focused on your destination. Look at the map as often as you look at the road." Our first leg of the trip was from Trouville to a village simply called Saintes. We prayed to all the saints in heaven for protection.

Testifying to Papa's brilliant choice of smaller roads, we were able to cover 276 miles in eight hours that first day, averaging about thirty-five miles per hour, which was extraordinary when you compare that to the clusters of people and vehicles clogging other roads. Luckily we were headed for the Atlantic seashore on the southwest coast, which was not a destination of choice for most people, so we had mostly clear passage and no trouble obtaining gasoline at small village gas pumps. Everything had to be paid in cash. It was surprising to see how many rolls of bills Papa would pull out of his pocket every time he had to pay for gas, food, a phone call, or a service. The vehicles held up extremely well. Papa couldn't believe that with all the pushing of the new little truck, he never had a single problem with it or with the Matford loaded down with its priceless treasures.

Many refugees at the time had no choice but to walk off on any road away from a battlefield and keep going. Many never had a car, so they were trundling with bicycles, carts, wheelbarrows, baby carriages, or no wheels at all. Numerous columns of people became so dense that they were incapable of moving forward. They would hurl themselves down in ditches if they heard a Stuka approaching. Women would fall with screaming children in their arms. They'd dart for the woods with no idea what obstacles might await them. Even if we had wanted to help, we could hardly help ourselves in the melee that was growing as we moved on.

We finally had to stop for an overnight stay and found the village Saintes in Charente Inferieure, but we had difficulty finding rooms. Of the few lodgings available, most were closed, as their owners were too frightened to open. Finally, Papa was able to secure three rooms in a small inn, and elected to give one to Bon Papa by himself. The second went to Arthur, Léontine, and Hortense, who aided my grandfather. Much to Maman's chagrin, we'd left our young governess in Trouville with her parents. And in the third, with two single mattresses thrown on the floor with grumbles from the proprietor, Papa and Maman piled in with all of us children, like a litter of cats. Space was of no concern to Papa; he merely wanted everyone to rest. And we did, dead to the world the moment we hit the beds in our clothes.

With a bad cup of coffee for them, watered-down hot chocolate for us, we got back on the road early but were crestfallen to find that all traffic south had been prohibited overnight. That's how decrees were declared: one day there was nothing, the next day there was a blockade with policemen at barriers closing the roads and telling you, "*Non*, you can't go there." You never knew what to expect.

The French government had just moved many of its offices from Paris to establish its center in Bordeaux, and they needed to protect the area with extra police reinforcements. We had to detour almost a hundred miles to finally arrive in Mimizan just before nightfall. This two-day trip of 453 miles with one grandfather, one set of parents, three servants, and six children, without any mishaps, was nothing short of a miracle.

No flat tires or burning engines, no arrests for lack of a registration, no loss or theft of luggage, enough gas to fill up the tanks, just enough food to keep us alive, ready cash to pay for everything, and barely any carsickness on my part. I just don't know how we managed. Counting our blessings, cramped from so much sitting in one position, we were stretching our muscles and unfolding our legs when screams came from Charlotte as she jumped out on my left.

Maman had stopped the Matford in front of our inn, and Monnet was waiting on the front steps. As Papa darted out of the truck, Charlotte ran toward him screaming, "Maman is dying! She fell on the wheel! She's crushing the baby! She's dying!"

# 16

## QUICKSAND

W hen he saw Charlotte running to Papa, Monnet called for the manager and rushed down the hotel stoop to find Maman slumped on the wheel of the Matford, unconscious. Somehow the baby's head had escaped the crush of the wheel, and she was howling in distress but unharmed. Both were quickly untangled, and the baby handed over to Hortense.

The three of them were able to carry Maman up to her room, and a doctor arrived without delay. The exhausting trip, the fatigue of watching the children, the lack of proper meals, inadequate pit stops, and the jarring tension of driving constantly in and out of traffic had so exhausted Maman that she collapsed on arrival.

Standing in the driveway, we were petrified, Bernard and I holding hands, whispering that she was going to die. Zabeth, ever the tomboy, was already throwing pebbles at the black cat curled up in the flowerbed. Fanny had run inside with Hortense and the baby. Monnet's wife hushed us and sent us to the kitchen for a bowl of hot chocolate and a *tartine*. Hunger overtook fear, and soon we were laid out to sleep.

Though Bordeaux was surrounded with police and soldiers, Mimizan and Biarritz, farther south, magnets for Eurotrash and surfing, remained peaceful and untouched. Sporting a craggy coastline backed by rough cliffs and pockmarked with architectural hallmarks of La Belle Époque, this southern Atlantic coast was well protected from

71

conflicts, quite unaffected by the turmoil eviscerating the country up north. War had not reached these shores.

By the time we arrived in early June 1940, summer tourists were stuck up north, their vacations threatened by the war. Generations of local families owned all the B & Bs, rental villas, small businesses, boutiques, and restaurants. They ran the place with children and relatives in the commerce of tourism on which Mimizan thrives to this day. A large natural park of nearly one thousand acres of pine forest separated two distinct sections of the resort. To the east was the village full of little villas rented summer after summer, and westward were the beaches of pristine coastline, extending for miles south to Spain.

Léon Monnet and his wife, Suzanne, had been living in Mimizan for nearly ten years with their two grown sons, who were finishing their law studies at the prestigious Université de Bordeaux, established by Pope Eugene IV in 1441. Monnet was director of the Papeteries de la Gironde et Tarn et Garonne, two departments (like US counties) concentrating on making wood pulp from thousands of trees in the region, easy to ship due to reliable railroad access to Bordeaux. From there, shipments were transferred via the SNCF, the reliable French railway system, to any city in Europe.

Suzanne then became Maman's nurse, always present, catering to her needs, and forbidding her to get up for anything but the bathroom. We were kept out of her bedroom, forbidden to disturb her for anything, not even a kiss goodnight or a morning hug. Maman said she had not felt so exhausted since she had given birth to four children fifteen months apart. She had no reserves of strength or stamina; bed rest was heaven-sent.

But after a few days of rest, she insisted on getting back on her feet. She consigned her anxieties to oblivion and focused on routine necessities. One of these was her dress and proper attire. The war could trouble her mind and maul her emotions, but nothing could tarnish her elegance. It seemed that this was her shield, a radiant self-defense, an impenetrable rampart that no power on earth could pulverize, nor would she allow it to.

Maman had her long hair combed and brushed and twisted up into a lovely swirl held up with a barrette or comb. Her makeup was simple—some eyeliner, a dash of rouge, and a brush of powder. She rarely wore mascara because she hated to have to take it off every night or it would smudge her pillow and spread under her eyes the next morning. Her lipstick was a pure red, never orange or pink, and not an electric, blinding red but a subdued, appealing red that enticed you.

You never want to think of your own mother as a sexy babe, but I am sure a lot of people thought she was extremely seductive. Men would sigh within earshot. *"Ah, votre Maman, Madame Gaillet..."* Bon Papa never failed to tell me, *"Ta mère est la plus belle!* (Your mother is the most beautiful!)" as she would pass near us.

Her dress was a simple summer frock made of cotton, often printed with flowers, and she had a white dress and a black dress for special occasions—church, a dinner—when she felt that a little extra effort went a long way. She wore stockings almost every day, and every day the same écru wedge sandals with a slightly elevated heel. Clip earrings, her pearls, and extravagant sunglasses rounded out a beautiful young woman. She was only thirty-five, and even though she had an extremely limited wardrobe, I cannot ever remember Maman not being properly dressed. As a child, I thought of her jewelry and attire as her own battle uniform, personalized body armor against the poisonous pell-mell of our world.

At the villa, Arthur and Léontine were well in control of their own dominions of provisioning and cooking, cleaning and doing odd jobs. Both were comfortably plump and had even-keeled temperaments, always polite, always smiling, always there, ready to help. They had known each other all their lives, coming from the same village up north, going to school together, marrying but never having any children. They would often say to us, "But we have the Gaillet children, and that's plenty!" We adored them.

By the time Maman was well, we were living in a charming Basque-style villa called the Gai-Logis, built in the forest area, somewhat away from the frenetic historic village and only a kilometer from the beach and the magnificent Atlantic Ocean. Life was unruffled and restful and felt heavenly compared to the frenzied pace of escaping Trouville and the disaster of Le Havre. We were glad to be off the interminable roads and tried to forget the miserable loss of our home and belongings. It seemed impossible to the adults that the Germans would come down this far south.

Behind our villa was a small, single-track tramline that connected all the lovely resort villages planted along the seashore. A Micheline ran several times a day in each direction. It was a very quiet motor tramway on rubber wheels that never ran above twenty miles per hour, as it went through so many inhabited areas. At all crossings it would blare out its two-toned horn, so we called it the *Pa-Pooh* and often ran down to the garden just to watch it go by.

One day Maman heard *pa-pooh, pa-pooh* blaring close by without letup. Intrigued, she left the house and went down to the track to find baby Édith playing alone in the sand between the tracks, the Micheline stopped just a few yards behind her. Luckily, the line was straight at this point, so the conductor had had time to stop. Our governess was then a young girl from the village, whom Maman sacked in a nanosecond. She hired an older, undoubtedly more reliable governess whom Arthur had met while provisioning.

Shortly after this incident, one of Léon Monnet's sons and his new fiancée were run over by the Micheline as they were driving across the track and were killed instantly. They were returning from Bordeaux after buying their wedding rings. Their deaths were an indelible tragedy, and the funeral, especially lowering the caskets into one enormous hole for both people, remained embossed in my little mind for a long time.

"Maman, where did they go?" I would ask. "Why is everybody crying? Why are they all wearing black, Maman?" My first encounter with death was so strange, like a different kind of Catholic ritual impossible to decipher.

# 17

## MAMAN IN MIMIZAN

*Maman was a lovely feminine fashion plate wherever she went. Her long light-brown hair was done up in a French twist with softening curls around her forehead, and she wore eye shadow every day with a dash of powder on her face. She donned lovely cotton dresses no matter what the weather and rarely wore slacks. She remained beautiful all her life, never gained an ounce, rarely exercised, and insisted her figure was due to two things: famine during the war years and multiple pregnancies, both of which taught her to limit her meals to small amounts.*

*B*esides reading war updates in the paper and listening to the radio a few times a day, Maman focused on other matters. After making sure the daily chores were covered, she would concentrate on locating the rest of the family and their whereabouts. The telephone and postal systems were still functioning on a fairly regular basis, so by calls, telegrams, and letters, Maman was able to locate her sisters and Papa's relatives and tell them how we had arrived safely in this region.

She orchestrated a clever buddy-buddy system, a chain of communication to keep everyone in touch with each other. Each person was given four other people to call every time some new event happened. If phones failed, telegraph. If that failed, write an overnight letter. This was a brilliant way to keep everybody up-to-date with family matters and war news.

Maman draped a large map on the dining-room wall and pinned little flags of different colors on it: red to show the German lines, blue the French, and green the location of all the people she was in touch with. A bigger white flag was pinned onto the top right-hand corner but it never moved. It seemed so high she could never reach it.

One day I asked, "Maman, what is the big white flag doing up in that corner?"

"That's for when we have peace, ma petite, that's for peace. When the war is ended it will go right on Paris."

"But Maman, how will you reach it? It's so far up."

"Ha, *ma petite*, don't worry. When the war is over everyone will jump to the ceiling, and from there, I will move the flag to Paris!"

Imagining her with the wings of an angel, I would often disturb her to ask when peace would make her fly. I didn't want to miss the moment. She would laugh, ruffle my hair, and assure me it would be soon, yes, soon. But I never saw her fly.

The white flag was Maman's beacon of a hopeful future, and I would stare at it every time I was in the room. It never moved. The top of the high buffet under the wall map was used as a worktable, full of papers, agendas, calendars, notes, and maps. Maman would stand like a general over her work zone every day, studying, ruminating, calculating, making calls, moving flags, filled with despair, anger, and toothpick-size flag-poles of hope.

It was inevitable that some families would want to join us. Maman became their real estate agent and found villas and rooms for rent for not only family members who wanted to come down, but for friends, and friends of friends, and then for refugees who began pouring in from the North, from Belgium, the Netherlands, Alsace, and other points. She refused to go through middlemen or pay commissions to anyone.

*"C'est la guerre!"* she would exclaim. "It's the war, and we have to help everybody alike!" And off she'd fly in her flowery cotton dress and high sandals to answer the phone or check on arrivals.

Everyone admired her. She became the Mother Teresa of Mimizan, getting to know everybody, including the mayor and the lawyer and the priest and the school director and the hotel manager and the owner of the youth camp. Maman was a bottomless fount of information with a large spiral Rhodia composition book full of names and numbers and contacts and references so she could, without asking for help from any-one, answer just about any question and find just the appropriate help for someone.

One day Antoine and Solange de Laage arrived with great fanfare with their four children and a gaggle of relatives and friends. The buzz of their arrival went through the town like lightning. It was as if today's most famous movie couple, Angelina Jolie and Brad Pitt, arrived in your hometown with all their adopted children and a large retinue of friends and helpers. The whole town went into a tizzy of excitement, and Antoine, forever the playboy, demanded an unfair amount of attention and reveled in it.

The noble family of Antoine de Laage de Bellefaye had lived for sev-eral centuries in St. Omer, just north of Blendecques. Though our large families were not related in any way, the de Laages and the Gaillets and the Avots knew each other through social and professional connections that predated my parents.

When that infamous bullet had crashed through our front door, Antoine had scoffed at our family for our quick departure from Blendecques. He and his wife had tried to demean us and called us *froussards* (frightened scaredy-cats). Antoine was sort of a chameleon, a nobleman who would play down his nobility with some banal bourgeois behavior, which always rankled Papa, who could only accept candor.

With aplomb and independence, Antoine de Laage had purchased a defunct sewer/septic-system business in 1935 called *Vidanges Inodores* (Odor-Free Pump Out), at a time when houses had small individual septic tanks and municipal sewer systems were nonexistent. Seeing possibilities in an old business established in the 1880s, he greatly improved it with bright green trucks full of filtering equipment and new pumping systems, whose final product was fertilizer for farms. This was a natural recycling service in its infancy. Emptying public cesspits and creating fertilizer from refuse became a well-known night operation, especially in neighborhoods where a truck operating in the daytime would create serious traffic jams. The rather fetid and plebeian nature of this operation did not befit nobility, and Antoine was ostracized by his family because of it.

He also owned a private bus service that ran from the ritzy residential district to the shopping area of Saint-Omer, permitting the ladies to go shopping together, without their husbands or chauffeurs to look over their purchases. It was obvious that Antoine liked mingling mostly in levels of society that could well afford his services. He was extremely popular with his clientele, who loved the fact that someone from the upper class was clever enough to cater to their lowly personal needs and understood what these needs were.

These activities kept the de Laage bank accounts flush, enabling them to eventually flee the North, following us to Trouville and then to Mimizan. Antoine filled up five yellow buses with fifty-two relatives encumbered by piles of luggage and hit the roads at their worst. Struggling to keep wading through crowds of refugees, he got badly injured when defending their turn to cross the Seine. He was still limping when he finally arrived in Mimizan where, of course, Maman had found accommodations for all of them.

By this time, Solange, who adored all of her husband's mischievous adventures in business, was fully apologetic for their slurs some weeks earlier. She became Maman's assistant and an irreplaceable partner in all the work there was to do. The two women found a common bond in their activities. Solange, the proverbial socialite, glued herself to Elisabeth, the anchored organizer, and soon proved to be an invaluable helper, always on hand to do Maman's bidding, covering for her when she had to rest, which was often. They forged a friendship that lasted throughout their lives.

Every day after lunch Maman disappeared into her bedroom and took a long nap, doctor's orders. "Madame," he had said to her, "if you don't rest, you will collapse one day, and there is no guarantee we will be able to revive you." She heeded this warning and never answered her door during her slumber, relieved to know that Solange could handle things.

Then in late afternoon she would spend an hour or two with us, whether on the beach, where she lay on a chaise longue, or strolling in the old town window-shopping, or just playing a game of cards, which she always let us win. We revered Maman; she was there for us and for everybody. Although her time with us was limited, that time was precious, and we reveled in it.

Within days of our arrival, Papa became absorbed with business activities but always reappeared on time for the seven o'clock news and dinner. Working with Monnet, sensitive phases of the Avot-Vallée paper business were unraveled. With their ownership of stocks in similar paper enterprises, they wanted to be certain that they weren't overlooking any hurdles or minefields. Being in a relatively accessible safety zone of France, they set up meetings with associates from Paris and local manufacturers' groups. Arriving by train with his personal secretary, the president of the French Union of Paper Manufacturers, René Failliot, could not believe Papa was in Mimizan.

"Émile, what the hell are *you* doing here?" he exclaimed, to which Papa with his slight smile replied, "I am waiting for peace." He puffed deeply on his Gauloise, smug in his assumption that we would be safe here for the rest of the war. It was not to be.

"Well, you may wait a long time, Émile. It's going to be hell before anything calms down," Failliot replied. "Now, look here. The North is invaded and impregnable, so you can't go home again. We have a very important syndicate we've been developing, the Group of Importers/Exporters of Papers [GIP], which is run by an idiot who only knows printing but nothing about marketing."

He stopped and looked steadily into Papa's eyes to ascertain he had his full attention. Papa just blinked and smoked, waiting.

"We need, we *want*, we *must* have a paper manufacturer like you to take over this group," he continued. "Here you are, doing absolutely nothing, so this is the job for you. We want you to head the GIP and stave off the Nazis from shipwrecking the foundations of our paper industry. Without delay!"

Papa stomped on his cigarette butt and asked a few questions, all answered to his satisfaction, so he said, "Yes, I will do it."

And on this, they shook hands. Papa kissed Maman good-bye, told us all to be good, to say our prayers, and to take care of her, and before we knew it, he was off to Paris.

# 18

## $\mathscr{P}$ A P A  I N  $\mathscr{P}$ A R I S

$\mathscr{P}$apa was gone from Mimizan to shoulder important burdens in Paris but, honestly, we little ones hardly noticed. This was the beginning of summertime, and every morning, as soon as we finished our hot chocolate and a thick slice of buttered bread with jam, we were off with our governess and stayed outside until lunchtime. We always had a governess, and this one was not another young local girl. This governess, with years of experience, could not believe her luck at getting a job with so many children when her regular families were unable to come down from the war zone. She was middle-aged, jovial, homely, unmarried, and a native, so she had loads of ideas about what to do and where to go, filling each day with terrific adventures that we loved to discover with her.

We explored the forest with its gigantic trees and millions of pinecones on the ground. We went to the beach where the water was much warmer than that freezing northern sea in Trouville. We waded with other children and splashed around, knowing we could rinse off under the cold garden shower by the kitchen. Even the seashells were different. We collected piles of them and made a little town of shell and pinecone towers all over the front porch.

We walked everywhere in the lovely weather, our little ears guarded from news of the escalating war. After a quick lunch of a bowl of soup, we all took naps, and then it was outside again for the rest of the afternoon until dusk. We stayed to watch the sunset, mesmerized by waiting and waiting for a mysterious green flash that people swore by, but we never saw it.

Papa was gone, but the baby, Édith, didn't notice at all. She had just turned two years old and, with her cute little dimples and crown of blond curly hair, she was content to go everywhere with us in a little stroller we took turns pushing around. She was always well fed, clothed, loved, and protected, blessed to be so innocent.

Papa was gone, but Bernard and I, inseparable, didn't mind. We were not even five and six years old and found protection and comfort in sharing games and stories, walks and naps. We never caused any rifts or ruffles, both of us being rather quiet children.

Papa was gone, but my sister Elisabeth did not mind because his absence gave her the freedom she was already lusting for, having turned seven that May, "the age of reason." No more scolding and discipline for infractions related by the governess to Maman. She was fast becoming a tomboy and scattered herself all over the place—in the woods, on the beach, in the village—and had to be called in time and time again, as she would never realize how far she had strayed or that it was dinnertime. The only one of us to ever have a nickname, Zabeth was to become a pack of trouble in her teens, but not yet, not here, where she adjusted to whatever was at hand.

Papa was gone, but my beautiful sister Fanny, eight years old, never noticed. Ever quiet and serene, reading and daydreaming, Fanny kept to herself, satisfied with a book or coloring pencils, making little pictures that Maman piled on her night table.

But with Papa gone, my oldest sister, Charlotte, felt estranged and dejected. She was fourteen years old now and had received much praise from Papa, who valued her burgeoning intelligence and superior studies. She hated our life in Mimizan that summer because all her favorite cousins were scattered, and none came down to join us. She didn't have enough books to read and couldn't share secrets with anyone her age. Often she was forced to watch us and thought we younger ones were too juvenile and naïve to engage her. Unwittingly, Maman pushed her aside from chores she now assigned to Solange de Laage, and envy festered in her oldest daughter.

Charlotte craved the extended family from Blendecques. She wanted a lot more than picking pinecones in the forest or teaching us letters in baby books. She and Fanny didn't get along, because Fanny was a dreamer, and Charlotte was a realist. Fanny floated around like a celestial seraphim, Charlotte was forced to play the role of headmistress. Six years of difference between the two was enough to drive Charlotte mad with loneliness, while forcing Fanny to avoid her like the plague.

With Papa gone, Maman experienced great pain. She was torn asunder, so much so that if you listened carefully, you might have been able to hear her heart breaking, like the ricochet of the bullet. Her physical cravings and emotional attachment to Papa transcended reason. She pined for him, day in and day out.

They had shared everything together since the day they had met. They had shared the exhilaration of a brand-new house on top of a little hill in the corner of her father's estate, and the grief of three dead little baby boys. They had shared the fear of a raging war chasing them into the shadows, and the peace of this little seashore villa in Mimizan. He was her pillar of strength, and now that they had found a haven without brutal German storm troopers underfoot, he was gone. Abject isolation and misery invaded Maman's spirit, and no amount of children or activities could fill the gap of his absence. No amount of patience or charm could pull her out of this misery, desolation, and sense of abandonment.

# PART FIVE

# 19

## FEAR OF FAILURE

When he left Mimizan, Papa had no idea of Maman's misery. He was already focusing on new challenges that required all of his attention. At the very stoop where Maman had fainted two weeks before, he had kissed each of us, lined up in front of him by age, Charlotte crying on the left, Édith smiling on the right. He shook hands with Léon Monnet and hugged his wife, Suzanne, urging her to keep looking after Maman.

Then he leaned into Maman and kissed her longingly but with reserve, without too much public display of affection. He held onto her just a tad longer then admonished her to work less and rest as much as possible, and off he went with René Failliot, president of the French Union of Paper Manufacturers.

Monnet drove them to the Bordeaux railroad station. They all three remarked on the lack of traffic going north whereas the southbound lanes were jammed and overlapped their own roadway. They had to forge ahead sometimes honking to make way, knowing how abominable it sounded to the refugees.

Failliot and Papa hopped onto the Sud-Express to Paris, where he then moved into Bon Papa's lovely and comfortable apartment off the Champs-Elysées, on the Rue de la Trémoille. Two days later he was named general director of the GIP. In this position he acquired a whole new set of daunting responsibilities. He was relieved to discover he was already familiar with most of the problems facing him, but he could not negate the fear of failure assailing him. He had arsenals of solutions and attacked each situation in an orderly way, several at a time. He was intrepid and aimed to overcome all obstacles in his path.

But his prayers were flooded with tears of confusion. Why did he leave his family? "Focus," he thought. "Focus and work. They will be fine."

His first task was to evaluate priorities in the purchase and uses of paper in three sectors: first, strictly for the army, then for the most important branches of government, and finally for the important private organizations attached to the war effort. He had to make sure these purchases were doled out equally among competent manufacturers, aware of their proximity to war zones. He reviewed contracts between France, the United States, and Canada, dating from before the war, but still relatively new to the paper industry. He was to try to refine these contracts without infringing on the strict boundaries delineated by those governments as well as those set by the paper industry itself, always mindful of the severe constraints imposed by the Germans as soon as they had entered France.

He later would relate some of this to us, always smoking his cigarettes, pausing to thank his mother in heaven for insisting that he learn English as a child. He worked day and night, seven days a week, juggling his responsibilities with the GIP, Avot-Vallée, government officials, and the German buzzards ready to pounce and swallow the whole industry.

None of this was easy. He excelled in the field of organization, and his talents shone through every step of the way. However, time was of the essence, because while all this work was going on, the Germans were moving closer to Paris, too close for the safety of the paper industry. Thus, quite without warning, all three paper syndicates were ordered by the minister of commerce to move their offices out of the city to La Baule, on the Atlantic coast, south of Brittany.

There wasn't a chance to countermand this order from the top. A huge convoy was organized to move offices, machinery, equipment, archives, and all employees who could go. By June 10, exactly a month since the Germans had kicked us out of our house, the convoy of thirteen trucks arrived at La Baule. But even before unpacking the first load, they were told that Germans might be too close, they must go on much farther south, even south of Bordeaux. Papa balked when he heard the name of a small town the government suggested. He knew there was absolutely no place there for such a carnival to settle in, no hotels or restaurants, no houses for rent, nothing. So he took things in hand and quickly made other plans.

Papa telegraphed Maman with the order to requisition absolutely every place available in Mimizan. After they passed La Baule, the massive convoy had been intentionally fragmented into several groups and dispersed into different directions due to the difficulties of travel. By this point, the roads were heaving with refugees, and it was only because of his formal Order of Mission papers that Papa and his group were allowed to pass barrier after barrier set up by the military police. They were forced to spend the night with the minister of commerce in the Château de Cande, Maine-et-Loire, surrounded by a bevy of secretaries begging Papa to take them away from the savage soldiers who might harm or rape them. A few days later, Papa found out that indeed the Germans did arrive at the château, but behaved very properly.

By the time they arrived in Mimizan, it was evident that Maman had worked miracles. As the convoy regrouped, everyone settled in.

Maman's joy at seeing Papa again was boundless. When Papa walked through the door to embrace her, she threw herself on him, clutching him tightly as if he were on the ledge of a crag, sobbing in elation in the nook below his neck, kissing him fervently. They held each other for what seemed like hours, and perhaps it was. Before long she regained her usual resplendent aura and personality. And it was only then that Papa learned of her grief and depression at his departure. She had never written a word to him about it.

But their reunion was short-lived. France surrendered to Nazi Germany much earlier than expected, on June 24, 1940. Before long the

Nazis occupied three-fifths of France. By establishing a line of demarcation going from the border of Switzerland and vertically dropping all the way to the Pyrénées, they held the entire North and controlled the length of the Atlantic coast. On July 10, the temporary French government moved out of Bordeaux and established itself in Vichy, in the free zone, under the direction of Général Henri Philippe Pétain.

While these major rifts were going on with different government factions, Papa navigated incessantly between Bordeaux and Mimizan, trying to get the approval from the minister of commerce for the rules and regulations he was setting up for the GIP and pleading for money to pay expenses and salaries. He ran into vicious fights between the Departments of Commerce and Justice as to who should occupy the magnificent buildings of the Chamber of Commerce on the waterfront. At a time when France was on her knees in defeat, the public squabbling of these opinionated functionaries was nauseating. While he could still get all the gas he needed, Papa's business problems were not resolved. He was relieved when the government moved to Vichy, and he no longer had to deal with it. Finding satisfactory solutions through other channels, his fear of failure in Paris turned into a much more manageable problem at hand: the overpopulation of this little village.

Inevitably, Mimizan was bursting at the seams with a tsunami of arrivals by the beginning of July 1940. Besides all of our families, friends, and the GIP people, refugees had arrived in colonies, and food quickly became scarce. The region was covered with forests and sand dunes, devoid of farmlands. The nearest valley, which normally supplied meats, vegetables, and dairy products to the area, was now almost inaccessible, as the Germans controlled all the roads in the region. Since all supplies arrived by train and truck, these evaporated by midsummer. Key railroad junctions were bombarded up north and out east. We had GIP trucks available, but their movements were scrutinized and restricted. German troops blocked any kind of provisioning to the populace. The weeks of mayhem that followed were traumatizing.

In the middle of all this turmoil, Papa decided to take the initiative. With the help of his personnel, he established a committee and designed a system of food ration coupon cards to be distributed to each person, with certain priorities for babies, toddlers, pregnant women, and the elderly. He took over an empty school and had every citizen register and receive a coupon card. As far as we know, this was the first time food rationing was ever established in France. The system worked well that summer. The cards were controlled, and the distribution was equitable. The quantities were tightly limited but sufficient to avoid starvation.

Life took on a modicum of serenity in our little corner, but elsewhere it was hell.

# 20

## TANGLED TRAVELS

One day in mid-July 1940, Papa was called to go to Vichy again to meet with the minister of finance for a difficult development requiring his expertise. Pétain's temporary government was now established in Vichy, so meetings rarely took place in Bordeaux. The longer drive was more demanding, but this was not Papa's first one, so he took it in stride. Nothing much was detailed in this request but that he bring his own secretary and a good typewriter; Vichy would supply paper and pencils.

The typewriter did not cause any problems. The new portable Italian Olivetti was all the rage, and of course Papa had one, but he wondered later about his choice of travel partner. He could not recall why he chose a certain Mademoiselle Chadroux out of a panoply of capable secretaries. Her physical appearance could certainly have made Maman frown at his traveling with *this other woman*. She was a showy, buxom blonde with rummy blue eyes, whose lace corset, barely camouflaged under a transparent blouse with ruffles, was loose over an abundant buoyant bosom. She kept her shoulder-length hair loose in a disheveled way that would not have hampered her on a pillow. This desultory manner attracted nothing but smirks from the women in the office, and the men noticeably avoided her. The strap dangling on the back of her shoe, swinging as she sat cross-legged taking steno in a short tight skirt, was a provocative invitation rarely fulfilled.

For a car, Papa chose a two-seater Rosengart. Easy to maneuver, black, and nondescript, it would divert unwanted attention. With a few liters in the tank, they covered 185 miles slowly but without mishaps, barely talking. That afternoon, during a short pit stop along a country road, Mlle. Chadroux found an apple orchard and picked a ripe specimen. Papa was leaning on the hood of the Rosengart, smoking indifferently. Bringing it to him like a smiling Eve, she extended her arm with a certain twist of the hips, an allusion he preferred to ignore. He had no more doubts as to her intentions that evening. They bumped into each other in the hallway as Papa entered the only bathroom. She smiled at him with a sly glance, in a priceless transparent nightgown. Her presence made Papa yearn for Maman that much more. He slammed the door in her face.

Arriving in Vichy, their silent morning ride severed any possibility of harmony between them. The white needle pointing down on the dashboard indicated a lack of gas, so their first hour was spent in a desperate search for the Red Cross offices designated to distribute gas coupons. The warlock in charge, surrounded by a group of women in khakis, was built like Hercules, strapped in a uniform so tight that even with the empty pockets patched onto her bosom, she presented an aggressive cupola. Knowing that gas coupons were rare and doled out in tiny measure, Papa did his best to charm her. Having noticed her name on her door, he regaled her with stories about his mother's friendship with her cousin Madame de Baillencourt, who were childhood friends. This rewarded him with a slight smile and enough coupons to purchase a tankful of gas that enabled him, accompanied by a melancholic Mlle. Chadroux, to reach the offices of the minister of finance.

There he met an old friend, Ernest Simon, who was expecting them and had secured two bedrooms for them on the same floor. After their meetings and dinner, Simon became the victim of Mlle. Chadroux's proclivities. She left her door slightly open, and he could hear her soulful sighs. One night he even found a note on his pillow: "One night, just one!" Neither man acknowledged her wishes, but their conversations often delved into women's foiled efforts.

Several weeks later, Papa ran into Mlle. Chadroux again in Paris. At his request, she had found a chauffeur to drive the Rosengart to Paris. He was pleased to notice that she not only spoke of this driver in eloquent terms, but she also seemed extremely relaxed. "Ah," he thought, "the pleasures of horizontal exercise will tame the wildest ones to a murmur."

Compared to Bordeaux, Papa found Vichy to be a turmoil of politicians, armed forces, journalists, businessmen, and females of all kinds, serious or not, looking for action or not, the whole reminding him of a Tower of Babel gone mad. All these people ran around with battered leather briefcases, looked studiously preoccupied but were really lost in confusion. Every large hotel facing the beautiful Parc des Sources was crammed with bustling ministries, but little work was being done. On his frequent visits, he was happy to find colleagues with whom he could attend stultifying political reunions and business meetings held in the large Hall du Casino, then go to dinner in a bistro, jammed with late-evening patrons and serving platters of consistently good food, to see if anyone understood what was happening.

The Vichy government was a shambles, the leadership fruitless, discussions endless, and results nonexistent. Instead of wasting his time lamenting this lack of leadership, Papa would make contacts, meet new people, give out his card, and collect phone numbers that might be important to his work in safeguarding the French paper industry from a German takeover. Soon enough he sat, with Mlle. Chadroux at the ready with her steno book, short skirt, and swinging shoe, to hear the details of this mission.

The minister of commerce, whom he knew only too well by now for his inefficiency and snobbery, requested that, accompanied by Monsieur Frézal, secretary of the Union of Newspaper Manufacturers, the two men should go north into the German-occupied zone to survey the productivity of paper manufacturers still in operation. They were given the important Order of Mission documents that would permit them to cross the line of demarcation as often as necessary. Without delay, the two men jumped into Frézal's car and took off on a road full of obstacles. The exodus was in full swing, the misery of the people palpable. Yet they were unable to stop and help. They had even been warned not to do any such thing, as many crowds were out of control, and they could be attacked for just a piece of bread or for the car.

When they arrived in Blendecques two harrowing days later, Papa could not believe the changes that had taken place since we had evacuated the house on May 11. He begged Frézal to pull over. He leaped out of the car, pacing back and forth, practically screaming to the sky, beating his fists on the outer brick wall and smoking like a madman.

Nonplussed, Frézal waited, then abruptly intervened. "Émile, stop! Calm down. I understand. But what's done is done, no? Look, we have an important mission here. You can't let yourself go, not now. People are counting on us. Let's get going."

Papa pulled out his handkerchief and wiped the blood off his hands and tears from his face. Silent, he swore to himself he would return. They walked back to the car and continued. To keep from going mad at seeing his house now set up as the German headquarters for the North, he focused on the work at hand and on the state of the factories.

It didn't take long for the news to go around that the boss was in town. Many of his employees were still in the village and could scarcely contain their glee at seeing Monsieur Gaillet suddenly appear in their midst. They gathered round him like a gaggle of geese, honking about their troubles, complaining about their lack of work, laughing about their children, and in general obviously appreciating the presence of the only man they felt could save their lives from falling apart. They hated being under the thumb of German domination. All manufacturing had stopped some time back, as they had no supplies and even less knowledge about how to proceed.

Though he was deeply distressed, Papa controlled himself and urged them not to worry. Seeing that there was some coal available for fuel and some pulp for making plain paper, he put everyone back to work and made sure the bank would give out paychecks as in the past.

Before leaving, he even promised that our two uncles in charge would return soon to manage the place, even though he had completely lost track of them. He could see the stress on everyone's face. He could only imagine the dangers of living in this occupied zone. But since there was no more he could do, he gave the workers all he could: orders to clarify their work and a modicum of hope. Then he headed off with Frézal, who appeared to be impressed by his professionalism.

They drove in silence around the occupied zone, passing many checkpoints run by trigger-happy young Germans, terrified that they could be the target of a shower of bullets should some mistake be made. Between stops at all the paper mills, they moved slowly, filled with dread of rumored attacks by desperate refugees cramming the roads. With great relief, they headed south and finally arrived in Paris unscathed.

When Papa found Bon Papa's apartment on Rue de la Trémoille still in good shape, he was overwhelmed with a flood of emotions that ranged from relief to dejection and fatigue. Though Paris was nearly deserted, a mandatory curfew forced everyone indoors by nine o'clock every night. Alone in the dark, he would rage at the ominous sound of German troops pounding their boots on the sidewalks, singing military refrains. He would hear this animated nightmare, horror commingling with harmony, and would cry himself to sleep every night, alone and petrified about what was to come the next day.

# 21
## MATFORD MYSTERY

*P*apa was living in a Paris now devoid of all its originality, its passions, its populace. He lived in a Paris under the scythe of a war machine brutally driven by an overwhelming power. Paris, the City of Lights, dark and silent, was no more than a shadow of its past, and Papa was in the middle of it when August arrived, and everything shut down. Driven by a deep longing for Maman, Papa took a train down to Bordeaux and found his way back to us in Mimizan.

He was relieved to find that all was well by the seaside. We were healthy, had good food, and were surrounded by friends and family. We played on the beach, explored the forest, meandered in the village. Even with crowds of people everywhere, calm prevailed. But he had a serious agenda in the back of his mind. He was very anxious to repatriate his shiny Matford into a private garage his family owned near Paris. This beautiful eight-cylinder automobile, delivered new in 1939 and kept spotless by Arthur, was glaringly stationed in front of the villa, as garages nearby were too small to accommodate such a luxurious vehicle. It was imperative he should move it.

Papa couldn't tell anyone about the Matford's priceless cargo. Stashed in old rags under a fake floorboard covered with a small Persian rug were forty kilos of gold in coins and bricks.

How this fortune landed in this car parked in front of our villa is another story. Papa had been in London just before war was declared.

He'd withdrawn in coins and gold bars important sums that had accumulated there from their brokerage firm. He brought them back to Paris without raising suspicion from the authorities and stored them in a vault at his bank. Then, he and Maman and her oldest brother had carried out of the bank little suitcases, each of enormous weight. Around the corner his car, the famous Matford, was waiting with a ticket for parking in a no-parking zone.

This gold represented a fortune. At the then-value of thirty-five dollars per ounce, forty kilos of gold represented over $26,000, but in France, where the twenty-franc Louis d'Or was traded at 4,000 francs, it represented about a hundred times his annual salary. And it was squatting in the beautiful Matford, on the street of a summer resort, in the hands of Providence.

Of course he had wanted to put it in his bank in Blendecques or stash it in his mattress, but procrastination and the war caught up with him, and it was clear this was an opportunity to make things right. He'd store it in the suburbs and deal with it when the time came.

With a late August departure in mind, and Paris as his ultimate destination, Papa found a good excuse for a detour through the South first. Maman's twenty-nine-year-old brother Antoine, six years her junior, had been demobilized in Toulouse. His beautiful new bride, Françoise Roussel, an aspiring actress already twice divorced, had moved in with us a while back, but her presence bothered Papa, as she had no valid papers and therefore could not go anywhere.

Desolate to see them go, Maman helped Françoise into a nest of blankets and boxes marked "Paper Files" storing all the family's silverware, telling her the smell of fresh leather would allay her fears of the dark. The would-be actress was locked in the trunk barely leaving a drift of Chanel N° 5. On arrival in Toulouse two hundred miles south, Antoine insisted they celebrate this felicitous honeymoon with bottles of cold champagne. Their tumultuous night in the next room convinced Papa to head out at dawn.

As he approached the dreaded demarcation line to reenter the occupied zone, Papa found himself caught in an unexpected snare. The Germans had closed down all main roads and checkpoints, diverting hundreds of refugees onto minor country roads. Set in the middle of nowhere, Papa landed in as small a village as ever existed, Orsennes, a hamlet surrounded by mostly grazing pastures in a region where animals were raised for slaughter.

Papa, a Gauloise as ever at his lips, fumbled with his Zippo, clicking its metal lid to subdue his nerves and wondering if he'd be arrested or the Matford impounded. Exhausted by midafternoon, he swung into a dirt alley devoid of refugees and, fully clothed, lay on a bed of straw covering a cracked linoleum floor in an abandoned farmhouse. The smell was of pigsties and manure. There was no sound but the wind, and he eventually dozed off.

Scouting for food the next morning, he noticed smoke coming out of a chimney and located a farm where a couple of peasants had set up a sort of public food service. For a week he joined other strays, sitting on benches at a big outdoor table and eating a succession of meat dishes at every meal.

Probing around, he learned that the cars had been diverted onto back roads to allow German troops to move on the main highways. Even with his *laissez-passer*, the officials wouldn't let him leave, insisting roads and villages were saturated all the way to *la ligne de démarcation* (the demarcation line) still fifty miles away.

By chance, he happened upon an acquaintance from the paper business in Bordeaux, Monsieur Lescop. Day after day they meandered around the countryside, the breeze carrying their cigarette smoke and conversations to distant paddocks.

"Émile, what do think the Germans really want from us? Just our homes, our cars?" Lescop asked for the hundredth time.

"They want bloodshed, Lescop, they want our land, our country, our factories, and our people. They have a patriotic commitment to Hitler, their monster. He wants to dominate the world. This is an invasion, it's an all-out war. What do you expect?" Papa replied.

"Yes, an invasion, a war. It didn't work the first time around. They tried with our parents, and here we are."

"Yes, here we are, in the middle of nowhere, and not going anywhere." Papa remembered Comines and his mother and sighed.

"So now we're going to be turned into citizens of Nazi Germany after all is done!" Lescop spat on the ground.

"No, we won't let them," Papa said, his own voice sounding hollow. "Something, someone will save us. This new German regime is so different from the last. I can't describe it. They are faster, more ruthless, and they're more cunning. What is terrifying is that they have no soul."

He sighed and looked around for some kind of sign. "We Catholics suffer from being so helpless. Make one wrong move, and they will shoot you. I have six children. I cannot take chances. All I do is negotiate with these pigs to keep them from taking over the paper business. It makes me sick."

A last drag, and he crushed the butt under his shoe viciously. He checked to make sure he still had some cigarettes. The blue package crackled under his shaking hands. Only two left in this pack; soon he would have to buy more, or he'd collapse.

"I suppose all that matters is our families are safe, and business is still unbroken…" Lescop trailed off, lost in a blank gaze. He took a last drag on his cigarette. "This is a nightmare, Émile."

"That's what war is, my friend, nothing but a nightmare," Papa said gravely.

Lescop stood there, looking at the farmland surrounding them, confounded. "Where the hell are we, anyway?"

When they finally received the authorization to go on their way, another problem suddenly surfaced. Barely a liter of fuel remained in the Matford, and there was little chance of finding a drop in the vicinity. Lescop had a small two-seater with just enough gas to make it to Paris. He insisted they go together—safety in numbers, good company on a long trip—and Papa agreed. The real decision was the safe storage of the Matford and its contents.

They found an abandoned barn behind a farmhouse where they hid the car, blanketing it with hay. With its large double doors closed, the barn seemed secure. The car couldn't be seen from the road. Papa locked it carefully, pocketed the keys, exited through the single side door, looked around—no one seemed to live in the area. In Lescop's little car they headed north, to the City of Lights, now a city of shadows, while Papa said a prayer, "O, Holy Mother of God…"

Apparently fortune favors the bold and the desperate. On his next trip to Vichy soon afterward, Papa shared a car with a trusted associate, picked up a two-liter gas can, and asked him to detour to Orsennes. They had trouble finding it, but after some circling on small roads, Papa spotted the farmhouse and barn exactly as he remembered them. Nothing had changed. He poured the two liters into the tank, and the car started; he waved to his friend and took off for Paris.

# 22
## PAPER PROBLEMS

*P*aris had mutated into a ghost town when Papa reached it that September 1940. In the loneliness of living in Bon Papa Avot's apartment all by himself, he realized how the world had changed in the five months since we had evacuated our house in Blendecques. At night, overwrought with despair, he found it hard to get to sleep.

Paris was deserted. There were no fresh flowers in the Tuileries Garden, where the trees were dry and drooping down. Watering systems, fountains, neon signs, and illuminations had all been shut down. Shop windows were blanketed with old newspapers and apartments remained shuttered all day, the residents living like troglodytes. No taxis, few buses, some bicycles. A few dozen vélo-taxis took over what little pedestrian traffic needed transportation. Curfews were obligatory, and by evening not a sound could be heard except for the occasional slam of hard boots on the sidewalks. Always in their vile green uniforms with black leather belts, high shiny boots, and stiffened caps, German soldiers requisitioned offices and apartments, taking them over immediately, regardless of ownership.

Other changes slowly appeared. The Germans opened their own cinemas for soldiers, which excluded the French unless they had a special permit to attend. But even with that permit the French rarely went, for fear of being tagged as collaborators. Nazis occupied the café terraces under balmy autumn skies and flirted prudently with French waitresses.

Personal contacts were highly frowned upon by their superiors. German marks became the valid currency. Paris developed an air of complacency, of acceptance.

The GIP had resettled in its former offices with all their employees, office machines, and file boxes from its different locations around Bordeaux. Their autonomy, however, had been clipped as they were now under the control of a German office imposing a new set of rules called the Work Task. The new director was Wilhelm Bracht from Mannheim. He was the president of a very important German pulp and paper manufacturing company called Papierwerke Waldhof–Aschaffenburg-Zellstoffwerke AG, still operating today.

Most likely picked because he spoke fluent French, Bracht was a lucky draw for Papa, for they had done business together before the war. Extremely bright and erudite, Bracht surrounded himself with assistants who came from affluent German families relieved to have their offspring off the beaten path of war.

A relative peace and understanding reigned in this peculiar coexistence. French and German executives alike participated in many meetings and often went afterward in small groups to a local bistro. If the occasion called for it, Bracht would take some of the top executives for a gargantuan meal at one of the better restaurants labeled *Nur für Wehrmacht* (For Germans Only), where there were no food restrictions for Germans. Unable to control his appetite at the table, Papa's stomach would later turn over. He never wrote home about this.

This forced cooperation between the French and the Germans protected the French paper industry, avoiding the worst disaster possible: a requisition. Great losses happened to other industries where the French refused orders. Factories were burned, people were killed, and businesses were destroyed. Resisting would cost everything. By establishing a minimum of acceptance and a semblance of cooperation, this status quo allowed the industry to operate without too much subservience and within the bounds of both governments' requirements.

Production had by then already dwindled to 50 percent of capacity. The Work Task tried to concentrate workers in the three largest mills so that all the other workers could then be sent to work in German paper mills. The Germans hoped to shift at least 70 percent of the personnel this way, some four thousand French factory workers, many of whom were middle-aged or older, very well trained in very specific departments and machines, living near their factories all their lives. Obviously, none of the French workers wanted to work in a German paper mill, and a cold war began.

At the GIP Papa was the big chief. He devised methods of agreeing to demands while undermining their results. He buffered initial demands and balked at requests to diffuse production under the pretext that each mill had its own techniques and each worker his own specialty. He explained that it was impossible to shuffle anyone or anything for orders for certain types of papers to be fulfilled. He made clear that deliveries were a lot more important than sending out some workers who would be useless in front of machines they had never operated. With memos flying back and forth, demands answered by delays, only two mills were eventually closed, which meant only sixty workers would be sent to Germany.

Papa carefully and secretly instructed these workers. Going to meet them by himself, he secured the building and sent the French executives out of the room. He lined up the workers and started with a prayer, then demanded total silence. Pacing in front of them like a general addressing his troops, he began.

"Gentlemen! You all are being sent to our enemy's motherland, to their factories, to their towns where they have families and children, much like you do here."

All eyes followed Papa's calculated footsteps, ears open to every word. "I am not sending you there to cooperate with them. Quite the contrary! I'm sending you there to do absolutely nothing, to practice passive resistance!"

Laughter began to erupt, but a grave look ended the levity. He stopped, carefully pulled out a cigarette, and slowly lit it, shadowing his eyes from the hot flame of his Zippo.

He inhaled, exhaled, and continued, "I'm not joking, and this is no game. The Germans have already marauded through our country, stolen our homes, bombed our cities, and invaded our villages. They have requisitioned and taken over businesses just like ours, but I'll be damned if we are going to give them our business!"

They clapped and cheered, but Papa stopped and glared at them, imposing silence once more. He held up his lit cigarette between his thumb and forefinger. "You see this cigarette, gentlemen? This cigarette is like a Nazi; you don't talk or complain to a cigarette. How could you? There's no language for communication between you, so you can't understand each other. And that's what I want you to remember."

His glance ran over the rows of men, sixty of them, silent, fearful of where this was taking them. "You will not understand their language, and they won't understand yours. Forget every skill you know. You will not know how to operate their machines. You will not understand their instructions. You will not bend over to pat a child on the head; he is not your child and never will be. You will not even think of looking at their women, never look in their eyes, and never speak to anyone unless they speak to you. And then, of course, you will not answer, because you do not understand a word of German."

Father knew his captive audience understood every one of his rules, and he could see them nod silently.

"Gentlemen!" he called out toward the back rows. "You are now stupid Frenchmen facing lit cigarettes. Don't forget that the slightest word from your mouth or the tiniest movement from your hands will burn you like a red-hot poker." With this, Papa threw the smoldering cigarette to the floor and stamped on it. "Give them nothing. God bless you all."

This passive defense was highly successful. Before long the Germans sent all these workers back home, saying they were all stupid Frenchmen who had no idea how to make paper and ate too much at every meal.

This was a major subterfuge on the part of my father. He was careful to never publicize it, for fear of being arrested for refusing to cooperate with the Nazis. After the war, Général de Gaulle decorated him for saving the French paper industry from requisitioning by the Germans and sent him off on missions to the United States and Canada to rebuild the business.

# 23

## PREPOSTEROUS PROPOSITION

$\mathcal{M}$eanwhile, weeks went by in Mimizan with little news from Papa, who was too tired and afraid to communicate any of his doings. Maman found life dragging by and longed to be back with him in the sweet rhythm of married life. With cooler weather approaching, and after much discussion with her friends, she decided to make a short trip to Paris.

She arrived unexpectedly at Rue de la Trémoille one late October afternoon on the arm of her now close friend, Antoine de Laage, who was more than happy to get away from the demands of his large family and many friends, also in Mimizan. They were in cahoots, and they had a plan. They went up north with the hope of pulling it off.

When Papa heard the doorbell ring unexpectedly and cracked the door open a tiny slit in fear of who might be calling, he could not have been more shocked. "Elisabeth? De Laage? *Oh, mon Dieu!*"

"Antoine de Laage?" Papa exclaimed again, staring at him with Maman on his arm at the front door. "What are you doing here?" He hesitated. "And you, Elisabeth, why are you here without telling me? And the children?" He had to stop.

Utterly shaken and speechless, he kept glancing from one to the other, back and forth, afraid to think of what was taking place behind his back. Why was his wife arriving with no advance notice on the arm of a pseudo-friend, a Brad Pitt look-alike playboy, both radiating with joy?

His head was swimming with conjectures, drowning in the worst thoughts imaginable. An affair? A divorce? An accident? The children! The family! His reputation!

He edged away from the calamity about to befall him. He went to the tiny kitchen, pulled out his favorite glass, popped two ice cubes out of an old tin tray, poured a good dollop of bourbon, added a smidgen of sweet vermouth, three drops of bitters, one red cherry, and stirred gently with a spoon handle. As he returned to the living room, his head was swirling. He took a solid sip and walked over to Antoine.

"So," he said. "What is going on here? What's this all about, de Laage? You just show up in Paris at my door with my wife at your side?" He stopped, his eyes wide and anxious.

Antoine reached for the bottle, served up two shots of bourbon straight up, handed one to Maman with a gesture that said, "Let me handle this," and with his usual flamboyant style proceeded to try to dissipate Papa's worries.

"Mais non, mais non, Émile, don't get this wrong. This isn't what you think. Let me explain."

"Go ahead, explain. Do it fast, and do it wisely."

"Émile," Antoine started with an air of flippant levity, "you've got the wrong idea, *mon ami*. We're not here on some personal escapade. And no, no, we're not having an affair," he exclaimed. "Look. Listen. For days now, Solange, Elisabeth, and I have been talking over the possibility for all of us to move to Paris and—"

"Move here to Paris? Have you gone mad? What do you mean 'to move to Paris'? This is war, don't you know? This is an occupied zone. Paris *is occupied*! It's full of Germans, for God's sake! This is inconceivable! Are you crazy?"

Papa realized he was losing it. He pulled out his Zippo, clanked the top open, brought the flame to his shaking Gauloise, inhaled deeply, and turned away.

"And what interest would you have in helping us *froussards* anyway?" Papa mumbled with a wry smile, still stung by the insult. His thoughts wandered as he half listened to his friend's absurd monologue, staring at his wife, realizing how beautiful she was just sitting there demurely, slowly sipping her bourbon, her red lipstick, her shiny lips, the top button of her dress undone. He sighed.

His friend? Was this a "friend" talking and gesticulating and offering a preposterous plan of moving both families to Paris right away, to an occupied city, in the middle of a war, at the beginning of winter? He had never been able to understand Antoine's motivations. He wondered…

Antoine was well known for his conceptual myopia and impulsiveness. It wasn't that he was unlikable, but rather that his choice of businesses was questionable. Besides, belittling his nobility through banal bourgeois behavior and his good looks rankled Papa, who thought of him as untrustworthy.

This is why Papa couldn't figure out why Maman had arrived without prior notice, on the arm of her best friend's husband. He could hardly understand this fatuous proposal that Antoine was trying to explain in minute detail. "Let's all move to Paris!"

"We are here on a mission to convince you, Émile, that a move to Paris at this time is auspicious. Mimizan is getting too mundane," Antoine was saying. "Here we are, already at the end of October, and there are no decent schools for the children. Solange has given us her blessing and can't wait to start packing. The three of us have discussed this project through and through, and that's why we are here. We cannot find any loopholes. There is no downside. We figured that if the two of us came face-to-face with you, Émile, personally, we would be able to convince you that moving to Paris might be possible."

"No," Papa replied forcefully, "it is absolutely out of the question."

He raised his hand to stop Antoine from breaking in.

"You have been living way down south in the free zone and have no idea what life is like here. Paris is an enemy-occupied zone and on semialert day and night. It is true that the fighting is at a standstill, and the war front is quiet. It's true," he repeated dejectedly. "And I've heard the Germans are urging refugees to return to their homes whenever possible. That's a fact. But our reality is that our house in the North is occupied by Germans. We have no home in Paris, the city is not safe, and we would be putting our families in great danger."

"Mimizan is getting too boring now that summer is over," Antoine said with bourgeois hauteur, "and anyway, we can always return there if things get too complicated. The rent is paid on the villas for a year. We'll keep some clothes and nonperishables there just in case."

Here was an aristocrat who enjoyed behaving like a peasant, who could recycle refuse in bright green trucks without losing his pride, who ran private yellow buses from elegant homes to ritzy shops and made every housewife happy, who ran a first-class service garage for their rich husbands' magnificent automobiles. He had no qualms, and he had no nightmares. He was like a politician, thriving above it all, letting nothing deter him.

He was also the kind of man who could bring a dream into the realm of reality, preferring white clouds to black linings. Somehow he was able to counter all of Papa's arguments and make him understand that this was, at the least, feasible. His meandering logic was incomprehensible but irrefutable.

Antoine pushed and explained. Arguing and deliberating in return, Papa came out of his defensiveness and began to see some possibilities. He was lonely. He missed Elisabeth terribly, and the children. They had never lived together in Paris. Why not now? Seeing his weakening spirit, Antoine forged ahead.

Later in the evening, the conversation turned from confrontation to vacillation. Eventually, Antoine got another drink, sat down, and stopped talking.

Meanwhile, Maman sat mute, enjoying the seemingly positive progress of the conversation, sipping her bourbon, watching her husband with yearning. In her mind, she was already making plans of her own: first spend a few days with him alone to reassure him of her love and fidelity and reestablish their conjugal harmony, then go look for an apartment not too far from her father's, should he come back to town, near a school for all the children, and something close to Solange so they could continue to see each other often. She knew to talk would undermine her friend's convincing scenario and might cause her husband to waver. She knew how often he pushed business in front of pleasure. This time she knew silence was golden, and she remained silent.

After much discussion that evening, Papa could see that perhaps moving us all into town was worth a try and said he needed to sleep on it. His dreams brought images of his enduring desires and brought up something deep in his nature. Émile craved to have Elisabeth at his side; he adored her looks, her skin, her perfume. To agree would bring her back. He needed her.

The next morning, with some reluctance, he gave his approval without wording his misgivings and apprehensions. As bright and savvy a businessman as Papa was, he was also a man with a romantic nature. In retrospect, it's possible that this was the worst decision of his life.

# PART SIX

# 24
## FOREBODING

On November 1, 1940, Paris was beginning to show signs of life. After having lost most of its inhabitants since the beginning of May, those less frightened were slowly returning to the capital, saying the Germans were not, after all, that ferocious. Fear of incursions abated. Cafés cautiously set small round tables and chairs out on the sidewalks on warmer days. Inevitably, Parisians sat there and read the papers smoking cigarettes, ignoring Nazis stomping by, moving two tables away if some sat too close. The weather was balmy, and the atmosphere calm. There were no alerts rending the air, no bombs cratering buildings, no crowds in the streets, no demonstrations, and no tourists.

The Champs-Elysées had fewer people going to lunch and strolling on its wide sidewalks, now deserted at night. Two theaters reopened in St. Germain with scant attendance. On Saturdays, children watched the Punch and Judy puppet show at the Tuileries with great delight, guarded by ever-watchful governesses. On the surface, life appeared normal for the French. Yet the Germans were gnawing at their heels, requisitioning apartments, arresting people for the slightest infringement, infusing fear like an oil slick, heavy blankets of eeriness permeating the atmosphere.

November brought with it a curious oscillation that guided daily life between occupants and occupied. Concerts produced by German bands on Sunday afternoons were cautiously attended at Place de la Bastille and Place de la République. People from the quartier, neighbors who hardly dared talk to each other any more, sneaked out to hear the music and vanished into their hideouts on the last note. Propaganda posters glued on walls said: "Abandoned People of the Republic, Trust the Germans," alongside others denoting arrests and courts-martial for meritless crimes. No one ever took a count that first year of the number of French arrested, tortured, and killed in this way. When asked for a number, they simply would reply, "Many."

Hitler had visited Paris as a tourist that year on June 23. He proudly had himself photographed in front of the Eiffel Tower. This display of power and arrogance near France's most significant landmark made people sick. He gloated about Paris as if the city were his own, while people spat on the ground and swore they'd send him to hell first.

Together, Maman and Solange de Laage, leaving all their children in the care of nannies in Mimizan, drove up to Paris to start the preparations of this ill-advised move. Crossing the demarcation line was somewhat chaotic due to the multitude of people trying to do the same. Papa had warned them that it could take hours. His own experiences crossing from Bordeaux or Vichy when the line was building up was less than encouraging. Nevertheless, because they had little luggage in the trunk or children in the backseat, and they could prove they had a domicile in the occupied zone, they were let through in reasonable time.

Full of optimism and anxious to get settled, yet with some misgivings at encountering German patrols in the streets, the two women went scouting for a residence. Eventually they found two identical apartments situated one on top of the other at 46 Rue de Bassano, in the eighth arrondissement. It was only two blocks from Métro George V on the Champs-Elysées, and quite near Bon Papa's residence. They liked the quiet residential neighborhood and loved the twin residences atop each other.

The round trip to pick us up in Mimizan and bring us north to Paris was stressful and full of trepidation. We arrived on November 1 in a circus-like caravan: two families with some friends, and several vehicles, including two yellow buses full of people, children and adults, servants and dogs, suitcases, boxes, packages, and various items saved from Blendecques, added to from Trouville and Mimizan. Some were daily necessities, some utterly useless.

As it turned out, with pressure from refugees mounting in Mimizan, Antoine de Laage decided to sublet our villas without consulting my parents, thereby eradicating any possibility of moving back. We had no recourse but to move to Paris for an indeterminate future of torment and famine.

Passing the demarcation line this time was no small affair. Questions from uniformed guards, Germans in green and French in blue, scalded us to the core. Why were we there? Where did we come from? Where were we going? And why? Were all our papers in order? Did we have a place to live? What was our purpose in moving? Why were there so many of us? Who was in charge? What were we hiding? It was endless, demeaning, and scary.

These and other questions kept us waiting for hours. I was petrified when they forced us out of the vehicles, pushing us back in as we tried to reshuffle to our proper places while they screamed at us. The soldiers were so huge, we thought we'd all get killed or land in jail. Helplessly overwrought, we couldn't even go to the bathroom, we had wet ourselves and smelled bad, and we were ashamed of our weaknesses. And by evening, we had run out of food.

Antoine de Laage, for once unable to control the situation with his optimism, was trying his best to convince the officials to let us through. Eventually, in the darkness of night, we passed like grains of sand through a sieve, leaving behind us a torment for others in the same predicament and a barrage of obstacles that dotted the dreaded demarcation line for hundreds of miles.

# 2 5

## THIRD-FLOOR JAIL

We finally arrived in Paris after an exhausting trip covering 435 miles in twenty hours of travel and many more of stultifying waiting time. We arrived in Paris, the City of Lights saturated with gloom, under the German occupation for this first winter of World War II. It was dreadful and unbearable.

At our new home, on the third floor at 46 Rue de Bassano, nothing seemed appealing or warm. The corridors were dark in this narrow prewar building, and worn-out wooden steps led up a spiral staircase to our floor. Immediately we nicknamed it *L'Escargot,* imitating the habit of French people who name all their properties by cutesy or moronic names.

The elevator gate was padlocked on every floor with handwritten cardboard signs posted on strings running through the grating saying *Hors Service* (out of order), certainly to deter requisitions in the building. We crammed ourselves into a tiny two-bedroom, one-bath apartment with Chiwang, our little Pekinese who never barked. The ever-faithful Arthur and Léontine got the attached maid's room with a tiny dormer window up on the sixth floor. Arthur often complained that despite all those stairs, he never lost any weight. He was a little rotund and very jovial. We never heard him complain about their room, the small bed, or shared servants' bathroom with no hot water down their narrow dark hallway.

The two apartments were owned by Jewish families, who had fled with barely the clothes on their backs, trusting a rental agent with their keys. They were identically furnished down to the wine glasses and monogrammed silverware. But they were dark and gloomy. Keeping the windows and curtains closed was detrimental to our psyches after all the fresh air and sunshine of the beach. Being small flats with no elevator, there was little interest to requisition them by the Germans, who demanded luxury in the city they were filching from the French.

On November 11, just ten days after our arrival, there was a massive student demonstration at l'Arc de Triomphe, barely a half mile from where we lived. Over twenty-five hundred students provoked the Germans. More than a thousand were cited for disruption of the peace, fifteen were injured, and 123 arrested. This outburst, which exploded and died down like a passing thunderstorm, unsettled my parents profoundly. They found themselves powerless, and Maman was clawed with fear. She refused to take us to school just a few blocks away, run by sweet nuns who evoked the wrath of God in every phrase. Frustration along with remorse gnawed at Papa for listening to Antoine and Maman. He clearly realized he should not have plucked us from the safety of Mimizan, but he was now incapable of retracing his steps.

The revolutionary students quieted down and went back to their schools. We didn't travel the few blocks to the school ever again. We stayed indoors, wretched, and tried to learn a few things from some books found in the back bookcase of the living room. I remember discovering *Le Petit Larousse Illustré*, a name synonymous with dictionary, a book I have never since lived without. This was the 1935 edition, the year of my birth, and I was enthralled by all its revelations. It smelled of fresh paper and print, every page covered with tiny illustrations of everything I could imagine, like birds and flowers and tools and animals; my discoveries were endless. With Bernard, I pored over the story of the First World War, which threw us into a panic for days, especially maps covering the same territories we had already traveled. Maman tried to forbid us to look into the historical section and searched for beautiful subjects such as costumes, châteaux, and flowers to keep us from crying.

Winter cold came through the walls, forcing us to live in coats and wrapped in blankets, of which there were never enough. Maman detached some of the heavy draperies to make do on the beds. We rarely had a chance to take a bath. A quick wipe over our skin with a cold washcloth and brisk toweling had us scampering for clothes and cowering for warmth.

From summer frolicking at the beach, winter became a fight for survival. Four of us slept in one bed, feet to head, two at one end, two at the other. Fanny and Zabeth shared the top by the carved wood headboard. Bernard and I slept at the foot, always curled up like teaspoons, bundled in our clothes and each other to keep warm.

Charlotte turned fifteen that November with no more than a kiss from each of us. She had her own little single cot that she kept along the far wall, under the shuttered window. At first she had pulled it out to the dining room to have some privacy, but when it got much too cold she joined us again. She rarely asked us to shush and be quiet, as she had done in Mimizan. We were becoming docile captives, fighting the cold and hunger. We would get an occasional burst of central heating out of the clanking radiator in the bedroom, the only one turned on, but so rare we could count the times per week on our little fingers, four, five—never, never more than seven.

Édith, so little at two and a half, curled up with our parents, hardly taking any room at all. The stove when in use heated the kitchen, but that wasn't much help as it was used only for cooking our meager rations. The rest of the apartment was gloomy, dark, and cold, and we hardly endured it. Our governess, a new one from the grocer's family, had a tiny back room, and I wonder still how she ever survived back there. We all used the same bathroom, and how we dreaded going there, the seat freezing our buttocks, constipation bedeviling all of us, so horribly embarrassing we would hardly mention it. We ate so little, how bad could it be? The fun of the seashore evaporated out of our lives as we became captives in a city filled with the malaise of occupation.

# 26

## ACCURSED MALEDICTION

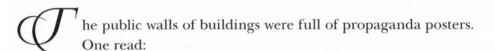

*T*he public walls of buildings were full of propaganda posters.
One read:

WARNING TO THE POPULATION
Shortsighted elements have spread malicious lies
through the population concerning the military
situation
and difficulties of provisioning for civilians.
Obviously these rumors are absurd,
but they can disturb the order
and the security of the public.
Therefore:
whoever provokes and spreads any such false accusations
as to cause a breach of the peace
will be condemned to penal servitude
in a labor camp for up to 15 years.
Signed: Superior Commander of Administration

This poster, in French and German, appeared on hundreds of walls in most large occupied cities, introducing French civilians to what it meant to be kept in line by an enemy occupying their country, their cities, and their homes.

Papa was so infuriated by their proliferation that he came in for supper baring his teeth. We were all still afraid to be loud under any circumstance, but Papa had had enough. "Superior Commander of Administration! Umph!" he snarled. "Let me talk to him, let me show him how to be civil. What right do they have? What is Pétain doing to help us? And de Gaulle?" Incensed at the growing control of the Germans and our inability to fight back, he forgot we were there, waiting for him for our meager meal.

Maman rushed to him. "*Émile, non, shush… les enfants…*"

She always invoked our presence as a balance to keep peace. She kept her worries withdrawn, touched his shoulder, and ran her hand down his arm as we had seen her do many times when Papa had reason for dismay. This gentle stroke of tenderness had always been enough to alleviate Papa's momentary discontent—until now.

"I will not! I want to rip those nasty threats right off the wall! A waste of paper! That is what it is! A waste of our good paper for these insults! Our blessed family product being used to intimidate and threaten!" He was incensed. Maman's huge eyes stared at him. He saw her fear that someone might overhear and turn him in for breaking the very law that was distressing him. He looked at us and saw how we cowered in fear. And ever after, Papa behaved quietly in front of us, as though he accepted that yet another edict had been sprung on us, and he had to remember to be strong while he burned with resentment.

Rules and regulations popped up to control the French in just about every detail of their daily lives, not only politically, but also psychologically. The enemy ruled forcefully and roamed everywhere to make sure people obeyed. Laws poured out from military headquarters and German agencies setting forth intricate, muddled, and unworkable orders, often contradicting each other, creating disorder everywhere.

Threats of many kinds were posted in the form of headlines, posters, ads in papers, radio news. Caveats were presented in many ways: direct, shrouded, veiled, scary, in print, on the radio, anything to keep the occupied aware of who was in charge and to force them into compliance. And those people, the French people, were subordinated quickly. People walked with their heads down, their eyes averted so as to never cross those of German soldiers on the streets. More and more, people stayed indoors for fear of disobedience.

The frequency of the irritating street checkups multiplied. German soldiers or their counterparts, the French *fonctionnaires*, would stop civilians anytime, anywhere. They demanded, "Are your papers in order? Let me see them. Hurry up, stop fidgeting, do it now."

French civilians always had their papers in order, deep in a pocket. The French, either blasé or scared, but in every case subdued and aware of who was in command, would stop and obey. They would silently stick their cigarette between their lips, pull out a worn-out wallet, and worm out their creased *carte d'identité*. They wouldn't dream of going out without it. They knew German soldiers and the French police were tough. Provocation could only bring trouble. Being without papers or even daring to show the slightest bit of annoyance or distaste could lead to an interrogation, prison time, or worse. Young males were particularly targeted to make sure they were not escaped prisoners or evading military service. They often needed to show additional papers, like a demobilization permit, an indispensable-work permit, or some medical dispensation that exempted them from conscription.

A person's basic identity card was as good as a passport. This ID card was designed with a photo and details like nationality, date of birth, residence, and employment. With stamps from the *préfecture de police*, the inquirer could easily identify whether a certain person was in order.

# 27
## RATION CARDS

*D*uring these long dark winter days, my parents would not let us out of the apartment. They were much too afraid of demonstrations, like the one on November 11. There were constant rumors that another could erupt at the slightest provocation. They feared we would run into patrols who would question our being in the street at all. Nobody would go out unless absolutely necessary

Our new governess was petrified to go out anyway, even though the beautiful gardens of the Trocadéro were so enticing only a few blocks away. We saw none of our family members who had not left Paris yet. Many had fled west to Orléans or south to Marseille. Many thought we were still in Mimizan and did not know about this inexcusable move from the safety of Mimizan right into the heart of the maelstrom.

Only occasionally did we see the de Laage children in the apartment above ours, but the less frequent, the better. Children's clatter annoyed the adults, who were jittery and skittish. We didn't feel like playing. The humdrum of radio news crackling in the background, the heavy atmosphere of melancholy, and our constant hunger weighed on us like blocks of cement.

Aside from seeing Germans marching up and down our street, we hardly ever saw any pedestrians from the living-room window. Early in the morning, housewives would sneak out to try to get provisions. Unless they were in a queue, group gatherings of more than four people outside were forbidden. Curfews were imposed and strictly enforced. The curfew time would often be changed by as much as an hour without any rhyme or reason or notice. Changing the times unexpectedly instilled fear and psychological control. It certainly deterred public acts of insubordination. To be in the street ten minutes past curfew meant inevitable police detainment.

The Germans demanded that French families return to their villages and their homes, trying to reverse the mass exodus that had so disrupted the country. But many homes had been damaged, looted, or destroyed. Parents placed classified ads trying to find their lost children and relatives, giving physical descriptions and the locations where they were lost. By this time almost one hundred thousand servicemen had been killed at the vicious war front, and over two hundred thousand wounded, many from families who never found out if they were alive or dead until after the war.

My parents would listen to the news every night, and their comments would reach us through doors ajar. Once in a while they would tell us what happened that day, toning down the most terrible parts, but wanting us to know we were lucky and blessed and, at least, safe. We were not happy, but neither were we dead.

It wasn't as bad for us as it was for so many others all over the country, who were still trying to find a place to live, some food to eat, having lost everything they ever owned. Our parents would tell us about them. So we knew we were not as miserable as our Jewish countrymen or the struggling refugees. Every night we would kneel around the big bed and say our prayers: Our Father, Hail Mary, thank you, blessed Jesus, for all of your protection. Amen. Bernard and I would cry softly while Édith would whimper in unison.

When they occupied Paris in the summer of 1940, the Germans had forced the French to synchronize their clocks with Berlin, moving the time forward one hour. As days became shorter and colder, the unnatural darkness added much to an already depressing situation. Long lines for provisions became longer. They formed in the middle of the night, often so long that some people just gave up and went home, starving. The stores never opened before nine o'clock and had few supplies to offer. Then they would close by noon and not reopen until the next day, if then, if any food came in.

Ration cards were established by the German administration to try to quell the wave of starvation beginning to grasp the populace. To get a ration card, we had to queue up for it at some office set up in a storefront. After standing on line forever, we would wait in front of a desk staffed by both a German and a Frenchman, each double-checking the other. After receiving a new ration card, we had to go register individually with establishments in our neighborhood such as the bakery, the grocer, the butcher, and so on. We were not allowed to go to shops in other neighborhoods or to those marked *Nur für Wehrmacht* (For Germans Only).

War ration cards were designed with tortuous categories and allotted to the population in precise classifications. Category A embraced most adults, those twenty-one to seventy years of age. These cardholders received the standard minimal subsistence ration, a pittance. We had five people in this category: Maman, Papa, Arthur, Léontine, and the governess. Category C was for farmers, T was for workers who had a job; both of these got extra allowances of bread and milk. Even though Arthur and Léontine were paid help they were not accepted in the T category because they lived with us in the private sector. Category E, children under three years of age, such as Édith, were to get more milk but less bread. Then there was the category J for juniors. J1 was for three to six years old, Bernard and me; J2 for six to thirteen, Fanny and Zabeth; and J3 for thirteen to twenty-one, Charlotte. We nicknamed our group of five *Les JeeBees* for years afterward.

The list of rationed food began with bread, milk, butter, cheese, one egg per person per week, fats, oil, coffee, fish, potatoes, salt, wine, and soap. It was then extended to meat, three hundred grams a week per family, and tobacco—one pack a month, for men only. Just about everything became rationed, even clothing, although it was nearly impossible to get anything of any kind at all.

Queuing became a way of life. You had to queue for everything at every store. No matter how patiently people queued, there was very little chance of getting what they wanted. Still, they'd wait on line, bundled up against the cold, shuffle forward a few inches, wait some more, and at the door be told there were only carrots. They'd take carrots, whatever was offered, six carrots, thank you, au revoir, and head bent, leave the line behind them to go home.

Maman and Arthur were the only ones capable of provisioning. They left before dawn and came home desperate and exhausted after hours of foraging for food with nary enough to feed the family for a single day. The ration cards had been distributed in October but were nowhere near enough to feed a family of eleven.

Maman was armed with the special *Carte Nationale de Priorité des Mères de Familles*, but it didn't help much. This special priority card for large families was designed so it could not be counterfeited or shared. The cover sported a wide tricolor ribbon imprinted from the top right to the bottom left corner. On the inside was her ID photo and a list of family members with their birthdays. On the back were official stamps from the ministry of the interior department of family and health, which issued them. It was printed on pale-écru cardboard stock. It was valid for only three months, and it had to be renewed within a certain date before expiration.

We couldn't afford for this precious card to expire, because trying to get a new one was a monumental undertaking, demanding days of scurrying around from one official to another. This card gave absolute priority to mothers of large families, presenting a pretext of helping the roots of society, the growing children. It helped, somewhat, slightly, rarely, but never enough. It gave Maman priority in certain lines, perhaps an extra gram of meat, an extra dab of butter.

But there was less and less available, and never enough to feed us all. Without recourse, we became emaciated by Christmas. All food supplies began to disappear entirely, and shops just had to close. *Fermé Pour Manque* (closed for lack of goods) would be posted on the door, often just handwritten right on the wood panel. The door locked, the owners disappeared, food gone.

# 28

## FOOD FORAGING

The interruption of all communications and travel between the North and South had now completely divided France. The occupied French in the North were entirely dependent on provisions from the free zone in the South. Because the demarcation line had disrupted all transportation systems, the isolation of the North quickly became severe. Deliveries of food were halted. Farmers either refused to drive their trucks across the demarcation line for fear of being killed, or the Nazis pillaged their wagonloads, sending their contents off to their troops. Vichy tried to promote the planting of gardens, but nothing could grow in winter. Skyrocketing prices and nonexistent supplies created a catastrophic situation for the survivors, who had only one objective left: to feed themselves. Our family was starving. Worst of all, France was starving.

Provisioning became a true nightmare. Maman and Arthur would go out in the middle of the night, long before dawn, to queue on lines for hours and hope and pray for something to eat that day. They carried worn string bags and old newspapers in which to put their purchases. In their pockets were their ID and ration cards and a small change purse for coins and filthy bills handled by so many who couldn't wash their hands. Nobody took anything but cash, and many places required exact change. The benefit to being forced to shop only in our own neighborhood was the short distance. Every morning they would walk the three blocks to these merchants, lined up along opposite sidewalks on one street.

Maman would stand on lines where her *Carte Nationale de Priorité des Mères de Familles* was most helpful for meat or dairy products; Arthur would go for staples like root vegetables or canned food.

Even though we were registered in each store by now, we did not have the advantage of being "established" customers. Such customers, who had patronized that store for years, could beg for a special treat from the back door. The black market was rampant, trading in back alleys, after hours, and favoritism from a shopkeeper for an extra two slices of ham was only for his "regulars." We were made to feel like usurpers, taking the food of our neighbors, who had lived there forever. When she showed her priority card, Maman was insulted by neighborhood women who resented her presence. Arthur got into fights with men in line, who asked who he was and why he was there. It took weeks before the grumbling dissipated as newcomers took their place and got the brunt of the complaints.

Léontine would shuffle up and down from the sixth to the third floor and always say how much easier it was to walk down the stairs than back up. She never left the building or went outside. Slightly puffing, slightly overweight, but with a strong solid body, she'd try to cheer us up, saying she'd cook something special if Arthur would just bring back a surprise.

To Maman's dismay, she would even try to straighten out the apartment, even though she had no gift for it. "I am just a cook," she would say, laughing and shrugging, "I'm not a housekeeper." But just as often as she would tug at sheets or misplace Maman's things, she would hug us and show her love by a special kiss on the forehead. Her apron smelled of onions, and the cotton was rough against my cheek.

Léontine was a shy young peasant girl when she first started her service at my grandmother's, and she seemed to thrive helping others. We were ever fortunate to be her "others." There was not much for her to cook from the empty larder until the two foragers returned at odd hours with possibly a cutlet, some potatoes, a root vegetable, and an egg or two. Then Léontine would get creative inventing some edible concoction.

At dinnertime, always at 7:15 p.m. after the news, she'd bring in the large soup tureen, with a long-handled monogrammed silver ladle sticking out, and announce, "Dinner is served!" Jolly Arthur would try to convince us that our soup—made from a turnip, half a parsnip, and a gallon of boiled water—was a divine cuisine. He would step up to the table and pretend we were in some fine restaurant.

"Hello, good evening," he would say. "What an honor to have such lovely guests here tonight at the House of Gaillet-Avot! I am Monsieur Arthur, and I am here to meet your every need."

I will never forget the way all of us children shared glances at the sight of those sad eyes behind his smiling face. Those cheerless eyes were sunken so deep from the burden of knowing that whatever they carried home on those cold winter mornings, it was never enough. Those eyes implored us to join him in his merriment.

"Oh, come on," he would push our bowls toward us in a most showy manner. "You must try what the chef has prepared for you this evening. It is a meal to savor. You will not want to rush through this!"

Between Arthur's sad eyes and our hunger, we were compelled to play along, but we did so quietly. We never replied in the same haughty tone that he put on, as most children might. Instead, we kind of smiled, though I imagine we were not much better at bluffing than our lovable Arthur was. We pretended as best we could and would put our thin little pinkies in the air as we held our spoons and sipped our daily grub.

It was hard to manage. Our utensils were heavy, the soup spoon so big I begged for a coffee spoon while shaking from hunger and cold. I remember smiling for real on the few occasions when "Monsieur" Arthur was able to present a lovely second course of half a heel of bread each. Seeing our sincerely happy faces always lit up his, and he would prance around the table, placing the tiny crust of bread down for each of us. Merry as an elf, he would bow and exclaim, "Bon appétit!"

Meat was even more of a rarity, but not much to gush over when a cutlet would show up in tiny pieces. Indeed, the bread was more worthy of "Monsieur" Arthur's ridiculous fictions. I remember well my skinny little brother sitting in front of his plate with tiny pieces of meat on it, maybe only four or five, when that was his whole dinner. He would pick up one piece and put it in his mouth. He would chew and chew on that tough piece of meat, but no matter how hungry he was or how much he chewed, he was unable to swallow. He always sat on my left, and I'd watch him with my dark eyes wide open, my mouth a sliver, hardly breathing, while he chewed so helplessly. Then, when he thought no one was watching, he'd bring his little hand up to his mouth, slip the wad, no larger than a marble, into his bony fingers, and carefully drop it under his chair, as if it would disappear.

Later I'd stand in the doorway, quiet as a mouse, watching Maman on her hands and knees, crying, picking up those dark-brown dry little meatballs off the carpet, sniffling, blowing her nose, and silently throwing them into the garbage.

"Bernard, *avale, fais pas des boulettes* (Swallow, don't make little balls)," she'd say to my brother when he did it again. You could hear the despair in her voice. She had already lost three little boys; she couldn't stand that she might be watching another dwindle slowly away despite all her best efforts.

My fifth birthday on December 1, and Christmas, came and went unnoticed, and so did the New Year. Why even mention them? January 1, 1941, crept in bleakly on the horizon as our starvation became progressively worse, and our lives were put in jeopardy, assailed by a series of diseases that nearly killed us.

# PART SEVEN

# 29

## CALAMITIES

We, the six children, were reticent and depressed, mostly lying around on the bed, staring out the window when it was cracked open an hour a day to refresh the stale air. Games weren't an option; we weren't even motivated enough to play the simplest card games. Some of us read, but we had few books.

Charlotte had a few books, but they were too complicated for us. Fanny would become eight years old in February, but she barely knew how to read because she had been pulled out of school at the beginning of such instruction. She always blamed her lack of interest in books on the war. Elisabeth had no interest in any kind of books at all. She preferred to perch like a little bird with Léontine in the kitchen, hoping for a scrap, or with Arthur, feigning to help just to keep occupied.

Bernard and I were like twins, just fifteen months apart, learning our letters and words together. I loved reading and writing right from the start. It was like a magic trick over and over again. I remember the challenge of discovering bigger words, of putting several words together to make a short sentence. I found solace in scribbling on pieces of paper. I'd run to Maman and show her the latest version of my curlicue initials, titles to my infantile poems, short paragraphs of my imagination. If she was resting, I'd wait by her door, sitting in the hallway, sometimes dozing off. I knew I was lucky just to have her there. Never minding my idiosyncrasies, rather than praising my fancy work, she would kind of hum, and nod, and suggest I should write in smaller letters to conserve the paper and use the other side, too, and the wide blank columns on the sides. How could I know of her exhaustion, her frustrations with our terrible lives?

I'd climb back on the bed to find my still-warm spot. I'd sharpen my pencils in a little metal sharpener that Bernard would lend me if I sharpened his, too, shreds falling on our papers, blowing off the graphite from my fingers. We saved the stubs down to the last centimeter in an empty pack of cigarettes filched from Papa's wastebasket, also used for marbles, bobby pins, and small stuff that could fit without enlarging the opening Papa made to pull out his cigarettes one at a time.

My brother and I were fixated on the *Petit Larousse* and focused more and more on the items we liked best: trains for him, flowers for me. My favorite was finding certain words that sounded the same but meant different things. In French we have so many of those homonyms, I could be occupied for hours, pleased by my wordsmith kingdom of unlimited possibilities.

Winter was harnessing cold weather with a dampness that reached deep through the walls and our clothes. In the midst of all this, Paris, which had lost two thirds of its population in the exodus a few months before, had gained eleven new inhabitants. We were now living with two servants and a governess on the third floor of 46 Rue de Bassano in the eighth arrondissement. Papa was often away on business. Even when he was home, he was so busy late into the night in the freezing study that we hardly ever saw him. All the responsibilities fell on Maman's shoulders. This is when we began to get sick.

It all started with one of us contracting chicken pox. One of the most common childhood diseases, it is sure to envelop everyone near the child who first contracts it. There were five of us still at the natural age for the ailment, and not one escaped it. It is a benefit for it to attack everyone at the same time, but there is a week of incubation for each victim. So the chicken pox hid out in one of us for a week then skipped to the next, then to the next, so that we had chicken pox in the room for a good four to six weeks before it ran its course through our lot. We got little bumps on our skin, we scratched, and we ached. A couple of us had fevers. As a whole, we were fatigued but came out of the chicken pox without scars, physical or emotional.

However, in mid-January, Fanny, a month short of her eighth birthday, contracted a bad case of the measles and became quite ill. Already weakened by the chicken pox that she was still shedding, and being a rather frail child to begin with, she succumbed to fever and malaise and remained listless for days until the fever broke.

Maman knew for sure that the chicken pox had come from a sick child waiting in a queue with her mother. She had tried in vain to avoid standing near her, but the queue was tight, and she had to hold on to her place. Inevitably, the infection had clung to her and followed her home to her children. On the other hand, she had no clue as to the origin of this measles. She dreaded it. Her medical dictionary spelled it out in black and white: there was no treatment to lower the fever except for cold compresses. Since we didn't have hot water anyway, this was easy.

Fanny's coughing and moaning invaded our bedroom with clouds of viruses floating on the air. By the end of January, we were all finishing, in the middle of, or starting with chicken pox, and now we were also coughing and moaning with the measles. Just like Fanny, we had fever, scratching, discomfort, and constantly desired more cold compresses on our little hot faces.

There was no need to quarantine anyone; we all got sick. Life was chaotic and crammed in this modest apartment. When Papa came home from work with all his worries and exhaustion, he refused to enter our bedroom and kissed us through a crack in the door. We were in the one big bed, head to feet, with the baby Édith now on the edge by the door, blankets tucked in tight so she wouldn't roll off, as she could no longer sleep with our parents for fear of contamination. Charlotte camped in her ever-smaller corner, unhappier in her loneliness than any of us in our illnesses. Maman and the governess were our nurses, both exhausted from sleepless nights.

We were cut off from the streets, the city, the rest of the world, but it didn't protect us from infectious diseases that crept in like zombies and attacked us relentlessly. We all got scarlet fever and turned a sunburned red for a few days. Then one after the other, we started to sound like wild chickens as we all contracted bad cases of whooping cough and drove each other crazy with enervating hacking heaves that persisted night after night.

In French whooping cough is called *la coqueluche*, a word that sounded so funny to us—*la cock-luche*—that it represented the only drollery in an otherwise dismal atmosphere. Sneezing and coughing into each other's faces, we all came down with *les oreillons* (mumps) and suffered through agonizing swelling of glands behind our ears. It was the last straw. The mumps made its way to us when we were on our last legs, barely able to get up, to swallow, to talk, to whisper, to breathe. It felled us like trees in a hurricane; we barely moved at all.

Medical services were nonexistent. Maman was armed only with cool compresses and aspirin. We lay there on filthy sheets in dirty clothes, awaiting our fate. We were weak, wasting away, moaning, and starving, unable to keep any food down or go to the bathroom. We were less and less aware of our surroundings, dozing in and out of reality, sleeping in the darkness of despair.

During this abominable winter of 1940–41, each of us went through enough illnesses to kill any child, but God was protecting us, and Maman was watching over us. By the time March came around and brought some feeling of spring in the air, we began to recover.

Spring brought a few rays of sun from the sky and fresh air from an open window. We could feel some energy returning to our arms and legs, coolness entering our lungs, and when we sat at the edge of the bed, we fell on the floor, unable to stand up. Little by little we relearned how to walk, to speak, to smile.

Spring brought about a few relaxed rules in the street, so we could go for a few minutes' walk, always to our favorite spot, the Trocadéro. Spring brought a few more fresh vegetables from the country, so our diet improved slightly. Mostly though, and so important, were the intangibles that came with spring: new hopes for our family and many others in the city of Paris. All news sounded less grave with nicer weather; people could cope better, and our daily routines were easier to follow.

But in the spring of 1941, as we were slowly rebounding from the depth and despair of illness, an unexpected disaster slammed into our lives. On March 31, Maman suffered a piercing miscarriage and was simultaneously felled by a massive heart attack. She was rushed to the nearest clinic in an ambulance, sirens screaming through the streets. Taking care of us all those months had taken its toll. She was now the victim of over-exhaustion, and the only cure was complete bed rest away from us all. The miscarriage had torn her inside out; the heart attack was almost fatal. She was ordered to stay at the clinic for at least six weeks of total bed rest. Her absence left us all on tenterhooks.

# 3 0
## UNEXPECTED CALL

When the phone rang on April 1, 1941, Papa picked it up, fearing the worst. It was the day after Maman had been carried off to the clinic. The doctors' reports had sent him spiraling into a bottomless pit. He had not taken a minute of rest and was so distraught, he could not think straight. With nerves frayed, he almost screamed into the phone. "Allo? *Oui, qu'est-ce que c'est?*" (What is it?)

His caller decided to ignore the brush-off.

"Allo, Émile! This is André Monestier! How are you?"

"Ah," Papa said, expecting a catastrophe and not a friend. "Ah, well. No, not quite well. Well, as well as can be expected, I guess."

Papa was taken off guard; he didn't know what to say. André, an old friend, seemed in a rush and went on, having no clue about Maman's condition.

"Émile, forgive me, we'll catch up with news later. I have a request. Can you meet me on the northwest corner of Place d'Iéna and Rue de Longchamps in fifteen minutes? It is of the utmost importance. I can't discuss it here!"

"Oh," Papa said, intrigued. Suddenly he had to focus on something other than the sorrow surrounding him. That corner was not far away. He could manage that.

He knew better than to ask questions after his friend's warning. Nazis tapped hundreds of phone lines, listened in on private conversations, picking up leads on various underground activities and resistance. The corner André mentioned was less than fifteen minutes away, it was lunchtime, and he would be safe in the streets. He had his papers in order deep in his pocket. He had no reason to delay.

Grabbing his coat, scarf, and hat, he said, "I'll be there."

Sometimes blessings closely follow disasters. Perhaps this is the Janus-faced order of nature. How, when life seems at its darkest, the brightest star in the firmament can fall into your lap and illuminate a divine door hidden in the shadows for you to walk through. This must have been what happened to our family that April 1, for it was not an April fool's prank.

Papa was at the end of his tether. He said so many times, "I will never forget that phone call. I will always be deeply thankful for it." He was sure it was that call that gave him the strength to continue to hope, that saved our lives when we were all so sick, and that helped Maman survive her tormenting miscarriage and heart attack.

He went to the corner wearing his old overcoat and dark maroon scarf that gave him the confidence of feeling inconspicuous. As he walked at a fast clip under gray skies and a slight spring breeze, he wondered what his friend wanted to discuss, in that neighborhood, on a street corner. At least he was reassured it wasn't about Maman's medical status, since André couldn't have known she was in a clinic. He figured they might have to meet some businessmen in one of the cafés on Place d'Iéna for a secret meeting outside the office.

André Monestier, who spent all his life in the paper business, was president of an association of paper manufacturers who worked closely together to keep the business within corporate regulations. Since the invasion, this group had leaned strongly on Papa's efforts to avoid being taken over by the Nazis. Immensely successful, a champion skier and athlete with a charming and beautiful society spouse, André was deeply grateful and particularly admired Papa's resilience and activities under the scythe of the Germans. Knowing many details from other paper executives, he couldn't stand to hear of our family's sufferings in Paris, although he couldn't help but wonder what had possessed my parents to install themselves in the middle of this cauldron.

At the designated corner, with a nod of welcome, he slapped Papa on the back and led him up the block to number 6 Rue de Longchamps, blabbing about generalities, laughing needlessly, as if they were on a buddy outing, making sure they were not being overheard or followed.

Instead of ringing for the concierge, he used a big iron key to turn the ancient lock in the heavy carved-wood street door, slipped into the building urging Papa along, pushed hard on the door to make sure it locked behind them, sprinted up three flights of stairs like a leaping rabbit, slid a smaller key into one of two apartment doors opposite each other on the landing, and entered a simply gorgeous apartment. Reverently closing the door behind them, his friend turned on the lights, while Papa looked around, amazed to see such a beautiful place.

André beamed as he turned to Papa. "Émile," he said waving his arms in an all-encompassing embrace, "this apartment is yours today for a minimal rent, for as long as the war lasts, and maybe even longer. You must move in right away; otherwise, the Germans will hear about it and requisition it. It is one of the last of the great apartments vacant in Paris. I am the only person who knows about it."

He moved closer to Papa and took his arm. Leading him into a sumptuous living room he said, "You are now the second person in on this secret, because I immediately thought of you when I heard about it a few days ago." He looked at Papa. "Your efforts at trying to save our paper industry singlehandedly are amazing, and we deeply appreciate your work. You deserve a reward like this, Émile, more than anyone I know. You can't stay any longer with that big family of yours in that tiny cramped space on Bassano you told me about months ago. You must take this place!"

Together they explored the rooms, all exquisitely furnished. Brocade ivory curtains were draped floor to ceiling, indirect lighting showed off cream-colored walls covered with magnificent modern art, plush carpeting absorbed sounds, all reflecting unbelievable luxury. Everything a person could dream of existed in this space.

This modernized apartment in a prewar building was huge, with at least eight rooms, all beautifully furnished, all in pristine condition as if the place had never been lived in. The living room and formal dining room, with a table and chairs for twelve, were separated by two half walls made of glass bricks, topped by glass cabinets open to both sides full of priceless bibelots. There was a library with built-in shelves filled with leather-bound books, several *Larousse* dictionaries, reference books, and many prewar works. The imposing Louis XV desk and chair should have been in the Louvre. From the entrance door and spacious entrance hallway, a long corridor to the left led to a powder room, four bedrooms, and two full bathrooms, all lined with ample closets. On the right side of the front door was a large playroom used also as a sewing room, and a narrow corridor that wound all around its walls to land in a huge kitchen and pantry directly in the back, also paired with a tiny bedroom and half bath.

They sat at the kitchen table, and André, in half whispers—though no one could have heard a thing through those thick prewar walls—explained further.

"You are not going to believe it, Émile, but it's true. You can have this apartment for far less than what you are paying at Rue de Bassano. It belongs to my cousin, whom you met a couple of times, the Count, I should say Viscount Bertrand Jochaud du Plessix. You know that du Plessix was my colleague at the paper conglomerate. He was a gifted diplomat, too, and was recently commercial attaché in Warsaw, where he dated the niece of a famous painter. Tatiana Jakovleff, that's her name, a Bolshevik Russian. She became pregnant, so he married her."

He shrugged his shoulders to dismiss such a misstep, and continued. "Her uncle was the famous Russian painter Alexandre Jakovleff. You must know of him. He illustrated the book on the famous Citroën autochenille expedition through China in 1931. He had a show on this book in an art gallery on Boulevard St. Germain just before he died two years ago. This is his daughter Tatiana's apartment."

André got up to get two glasses of water from the tap and returned to his chair. "Lucky the Germans haven't poisoned our water yet!" he exclaimed.

Papa noticed that the sink was like new, not the old-fashioned white porcelain kind often spotted with rust marks. He admired the glossy white cabinets with glass doors, full of glasses and dishes, the new linoleum floor, the large double window above the sink. Glancing out he saw a square courtyard lined with green flower boxes hanging on windowsills, dark soil bereft of plantings now. A small fountain with a white marble statue of a nymph in the center had also lost its spouting water, and was surrounded with colored outdoor tiles laid in perfect symmetry. He turned and leaned back on the edge, waiting for more. He thought he was living in a dream when he noticed André looking at him and getting more serious.

"Ah," he said for lack of words. "And where is this Tatiana today?"

# 31
## PLANE CRASH

"Émile, listen to me," André said. "Sit down, relax."

Once their eyes were locked, he continued. "This is important, about the apartment. When the war broke out, Bertrand was in Morocco and heard the call for mobilization sent out by de Gaulle. He decided to join de Gaulle in London when Pétain went to Vichy. He was a sublieutenant in the Free French Air Force, and in Casablanca he was able to commandeer a small tourist plane with a couple of friends. But flying over Gibraltar, his plane was attacked by some trigger-happy Spaniards who had no idea this was a friendly aircraft. The plane was hit and went down in flames. Losing Bertrand like that has affected all of us who knew him. A stupid accident, brutal, needless, and the loss of a great man."

Shaking his head, he stopped for a minute, and then his voice changed to a more bitter tone. It was clear he didn't approve of his cousin's choice in the matter of women, especially not this latest one. "The young widow, Tatiana, did not wait around too long. She called me last week and took off for New York, where she has a lover, Alexander Lieberman. He is also Russian, from Kiev, an artist of some kind. Turns out they knew each other as kids back in Russia, though Tatiana is seven years older than he is. Terribly handsome, I hear. Anyway, they are both Jewish, so they cannot come back, of course. This is her apartment, now that Bertrand is dead! She trusted me with finding somebody who can protect it with their heart and soul, keep it safe from being requisitioned. I think you are the one. I cannot think of anyone more deserving. Émile, tell me, answer me."

He stopped and looked Papa in the eye. He waited, filling the silence with a prayer, wanting a positive answer.

"Ah," Papa said again. It took him a while to open up. "Somebody to protect it? This is like a museum. You need a monk or a lawyer to keep it in this condition."

"No, Émile, I want you! I immediately thought of you. We need a regular presence in it, an unquestionable tenant, someone like you and Elisabeth and your chain of children to fill it up. How is she, by the way? And the children? Are they all OK? No one else deserves it more than you do. You must take it!"

He was too impatient to wait for answers and started pacing. Papa was truly astounded. He opened his mouth to say something about his wife and closed it without uttering a word. To bring up her medical condition now would be to shatter this dream, he would explain later. Nothing like this had ever happened to him. This was a gift from heaven. How could he refuse?

Yet, he was a little afraid. He had made such a stupid move bringing us up to Paris from Mimizan. What was the catch here? He could only think of the obvious. "André, I have six children, and a governess, and Arthur and Léontine to think of. This is like a museum, I don't want them to wreck the place…"

"I know, I know," André exclaimed. "They won't. That's why I want you to take this apartment. I don't know of anyone more responsible in such dire straits as your family, that's why you would fit perfectly here. I know your children, they are like little saints, so well behaved, so quiet. Did you see all the rooms? You can put all the artwork in the library and lock the doors if you want. But I'm sure you won't have to, your children can be warned to be careful. There is no artwork in the kids' rooms, just plain furniture. She has only the one daughter you know, Francine, still only a tiny tot. I know Elisabeth and the governess can keep yours in hand. I haven't shown it to you yet, but the servants' quarters upstairs are available too, for your couple, with a private bathroom, no less." He looked sideways at Papa and quipped, "This is Longchamps, Émile, not Bassano."

Papa nodded, hardly registering the slight, then asked several questions to steady his heartbeat—this was no time to have a heart attack!

How many people were in on this? None.

Would it be legal for him to move in? Yes.

What about drawbacks, negatives, unseen problems? No, no, none of that.

How long a lease was required? None, no lease at all, just month-to-month payments to a lawyer at his office, no paperwork but a contract to show he was legally there.

There were no obstacles, no encumbrances. A simple yes would make it Papa's. This mirage would be his to live in.

André reassured him that everything was in order. He had permission from the owner, Tatiana Jakovleff du Plessix, in writing. They shared the same attorney. He would take care of all the paperwork. It was minimal and could be handled overnight. Here were the keys; all he had to do was move in as soon as possible.

Papa, still in a daze, nodded his agreement. They shook hands and agreed to meet the next day to finalize all the details.

The only real warning André gave Papa was this: "Émile, be very careful when you go from one apartment to the other. You must do it as if it was not happening at all. You can't raise the suspicions of anyone, from the concierges to the patrols. Don't talk to any of the shopkeepers until you've taken over the apartment and vacated the other. If anyone gets wind of this move, you could be in great trouble, and Tatiana could lose her apartment. But I trust you; you are one of the smartest men I've ever met. I should say *the* smartest except for being in Paris at this time with such a big family in such a tiny apartment at Bassano! Anyway, this place will decompress you. I know you'll figure out a way to do this without a hitch. Good luck!"

After they signed the papers and shook hands the next day, they parted, and Papa found a direct bus line to Neuilly, where he went straight to Maman's bedside in the little clinic on the Boulevard du Château. First he made sure she was comfortable, that she felt better. He could see that, in spite of being feeble and pale, she was recuperating. Then he walked around, made sure no one was within earshot, closed the door, and pulled up a chair close to her bedside. Slowly, he whispered the whole story to her.

In telling it in his own voice, he started to realize that this was real, an exceptional offer. His growing excitement carried to her as he squeezed her hand. "I am sure it will be all right, *ma chérie*. I met with André and the lawyer. We could find no loopholes or problems. We can occupy the apartment all during the war, and possibly longer. Apparently this woman, Tatiana, is well settled in New York with her lover. Mostly I'll have to be very careful with the move."

Now that this miracle was becoming reality, Papa wouldn't be intimidated, no matter what happened. He could persuade anyone in his way that nothing unusual was happening. He finished talking by repeating André's warning about the move.

"What do you think, Elisabeth? Do you think we can do it? Do you think it will work?"

Maman reassured him it would all go fine as long as he was careful. She trusted him completely. She was so delighted he wasn't mad at her for losing another baby. She wanted to get back into his confidence, she needed to find new strength. She wanted peace.

"Oh, Émile," she whispered, "what a blessing, what a godsend. I'll be better soon, and I'll be there for you." She squeezed his hand softly and dozed off with a smile on her face. Good news was more efficient than any medicine, and sleep would cure her worries.

# 3 2

## $S$ UBTERFUGE

With no time to waste, Papa put everything in motion. In retrospect, the move from 46 Rue de Bassano to 6 Rue de Longchamps, all of one kilometer, three-fifths of a mile, a ten-minute walk in the middle of occupied Paris, was quite a subterfuge. His plan of action to hide his true objective and evade any unpleasant situation obsessed Papa for the next few days. Much later we would share our memories as if we had been part of an uproarious farce, full of chaos and intrigue, and we laughed over it a million times.

We would remember bits and pieces and regale each other with details. Each of us had a part in it. With the regimentation and discipline embedded into us by relatives, governesses, and illnesses, we followed orders like troopers. Maman was upset to have missed it all, but deeply thankful to be released to our new home a few weeks later and to find it so heavenly. How it all happened so fast is still a mystery to all of us.

Paris was the center of a tightly occupied war zone, entirely governed by the Nazis, where everything was suspect and everyone untrustworthy. The slightest abnormal movement of any kind could be reported. Nazi soldiers and French police spied on every French citizen. French citizens spied on all their neighbors. The concierges in the *rez-de-chaussée* (ground-floor) apartments of each building were the worst. They spied on everyone through their curtains in the entrance hall and from their windows on the street. They demanded payoffs for any infringement in their building and expected a reward for not giving tips to the police. No one could be trusted. Yet time was of the essence; we had to move immediately.

Subterfuge, evasion, hiding, connivance, trickery, elusiveness, tips, payoffs, minute preparations, and planning all went into this unusual act of heroism Papa had to deploy to move us. He knew some of these acts were against his religion, and he knew God and André would never forgive him if he got caught. A single gaffe could send us all to jail. A denouncement could result in hours of questioning by the police. A sneeze or a cough at the wrong time could ruin the whole plan. But God was on our side and gave Papa all the inspiration he needed to do things right.

The lucky part was that we had no furniture to move. The difficult part was moving all the suitcases and boxes unnoticed. We didn't have that much, but still, getting six emaciated children, hardly able to walk, to carry something from one place to the other was no easy feat. Although he had some at his disposal, a truck was out of the question, as it would be too big and visible.

Like an army commander, Papa wrote out scenario after scenario and finally devised a sort of relay move where only bits and pieces would go over from time to time, alternating one child here, a bag there, a car driven by André with some things in the trunk a little later, one thing at a time, not too many in one day, yet enough so that this wouldn't last for days and raise suspicions.

Once on the way, there was to be no hesitation; one had to go forward and not look back. Each time one of us walked out of the building, we stood on the verge of the unknown. Whatever challenges we faced, we had to overcome them. He showed us how to look straight forward, how to breathe calmly, how to focus on the target, not dwell on what might happen, and never—never—look a soldier in the eye. We learned to be invisible, to keep anyone from seeing us at all. We were well aware that this was not a street in Mimizan but a guarded city in the hands of an enemy. We had been denied many things since the start of the war, but we had discipline in our blood. Whatever Papa said, we obeyed.

Our governess was the one most petrified. Fear can be paralyzing and so infectious. Like a bacteria, it spreads from one person to another more quickly than a fever. She didn't have the kind of character that kept Arthur and Léontine prepared each time they were asked to perform. She had to be tamed and guided.

Charlotte, who was fifteen, was put in charge of keeping her in line. She relished the responsibility and took it quite in stride. She put on her strict-looking school uniform, crammed all she could into her backpack, carried a few books on one arm, held the hand of the governess in the other, and, looking straight ahead, off they went at ten one morning, with the second hand of the governess on the loaded shopping cart on two wheels behind them.

Charlotte was a natural guide. She made sure to stop at red lights before crossing a street. She would throw a solicitous glance toward the woman she was guiding, making believe she was an invalid. She planned her route carefully with the help of Papa. Instead of following the slightly shorter route down the elegant wide Avenue Pierre 1er de Serbie through the huge Place d'Iéna where troops were more likely to patrol, she picked the narrow Rue de Bassano, followed the no wider Rue de Lubeck, cut left on Rue de Longchamps, and went down to our new building.

She carried herself so well that Papa decided she then had to get the baby Édith over, since the governess was hopeless, and Maman was not there yet. If Maman had known of his plan, she would never have accepted it: a fifteen-year-old pushing a two-year-old in a stroller full of hidden supplies in every pocket and under a diaper in a city full of enemies. Charlotte herself had her backpack refilled, too, and felt like a champion relating the story to Maman when she came home sometime later. Not to mention the pride she felt at Papa's approval, something he rarely showed.

Moving into a gorgeous and spacious first-class apartment improved our lives immeasurably. The building had better heating, and the elevator worked. We had more bedrooms, more beds, more linens and blankets, more space everywhere, and Maman was finally coming home. We only craved some food to eat.

# 33
## LUXURY IN LIMBO

When Maman came home from the clinic, she was overjoyed at the commodious layout, impressed by the unusual modern art collection, and deeply grateful for the numerous rooms to disperse us. She needed ample rest and couldn't marshal her responsibilities as before. She had lost weight, and her strength had evaporated with it. She loved our great adventure stories of the move from Bassano. It took her such a long time to convalesce that Papa was quite concerned, but his anxiety was mellowed by our happiness at having her home. Her presence and a glorious new spring imbued our walls with an aura of peace.

By the end of May, we were fully settled in our new apartment. This lovely street was lined with trees and elegant buildings that dated back to the turn of the century. It was bookended by the busy cafés, brasseries, and boutiques of the Place d'Iéna on the southern end and a forsaken strip of discarded slums and squatters on the north, an abandoned site of old city walls that had been destroyed in World War I. They were two different worlds, and we lived between them, luckily closer to the better.

To be at No. 6, close to the Trocadéro, was to be in the right location. This was the prime residential neighborhood of Paris, elegant, refined, rich, and pretentious. We were not of that ilk. We were nearly broke, nearly dead, deprived children bereft of an education. We were old school, middle-class, and barely alive. We were protected as long as we didn't go anywhere, and we appreciated that the apartment was agreeably posh. If we were going to die, we would do so lying on a plush couch, arms akimbo in a queen-size bed, or buried in deep wool carpeting.

At first, things were looking up. The balmy spring and small breezes brought warmth into the windows of the apartment so that June was comfortable. While we withered from malnourishment, we improved as we shook off microbes and diseases like a butterfly sheds its cocoon. Maman was up and at it again, at least in the morning in the queues. She and Arthur had become adept at queuing at food stores at five o'clock.

The storekeepers in our new neighborhood were just as snobbish as their patrons, but they could recognize a true character when they met one. They quickly adopted Arthur and adored his jocular nature. He always had a good word for them and remembered their names. He hadn't shed any noticeable weight despite the circumstances, which Madame Lépic at the dairy market would tease him about and slip him a few extra ounces of cheese or a quart of milk. "Ah, Madame," he would whisper, planting a kiss on her red cheek, "*Comme je vous aime* (How grateful I am)," much to her satisfaction.

They also began to recognize Maman with her priority card and take pity on her, so skinny, marvelously well dressed, but never extravagant. Sometimes she'd get an extra potato or cutlet, a couple of carrots or beets. Sometimes she even took Bernard by the hand, like the beggars in Morocco with their kids pulling your skirt, to beg for more, to soften the heart of the shopkeeper, who'd shake his head at the pathetic little boy and try to slip something in her basket without others noticing his kind gesture.

The trend of our lives in the luxury apartment was easy, going to bed as early as possible, waking as late as we could, and staying occupied with the limited number of activities at our disposal. We stopped trying to invent things to do and played endless card games with no regard to cheating or winning. We rolled colorful glass marbles up and down the long hallway to the kitchen, which ruffled Léontine to no end, always afraid to snap her ankle on one of them. We told her she should get roller skates instead of carrying dishes for miles and miles to the dining room.

We leafed with great care through some priceless art books left on the living room coffee table, though we had been warned not to touch anything. One day they were relegated to a high shelf in an obscure closet.

In the sewing room there was a large antique armoire with carved double doors, tightly locked. I would run my fingers along the carvings, tracing its intricate whittles. Maman caught me one day, and after that the doors to the sewing room were locked as well.

That big armoire represented to me all that was hope and mystery in our childhood. Tatiana had it filled with all her little daughter's toys and had forbidden access to it. For a child so young, with no toys at all, to know that just beyond a locked door there was a mass of them, well, it lured me to it every time the room was open. But, like my childhood, that armoire had been locked, and its contents made unattainable.

Outside, the war was raging on several fronts. Poland had been invaded in 1939, followed by Norway in April 1940 and France in May. Hitler was not letting up his attacks all over Europe. In 1941 he attacked Yugoslavia and Greece in April, Crete in May, and then proceeded to invade Russia on June 22. Every day the news reported a fresh disaster.

Children like us, living under the occupation, survived in a manner few can comprehend. No words can convey the terror of a *blitzkrieg*. People fleeing in front of advancing troops watched their cities bombed and incinerated. Stuka bullets randomly ripped through the innocent. Getting shot by a farmer for stealing apples was equally possible. Parents, uncertain if their child had been shot or merely lost on a teeming road of frantic exiles, collapsed from despair and surrendered their last breath to hopelessness. We were in the occupied zone, and we were in danger if we stepped out the front door.

Our parents would repeat to us, "Yes, we are unfortunate, but we are not enduring the worst." Papa wanted us to remember that like a mantra, as if he were reassuring himself that he had not completely failed us.

He would relate some of his crossings of the demarcation line and how families were torn apart, even murdered. He had, at least, been able to secure for us the guise of comfort.

He wanted us to understand why our country was not helping its people. He explained how the Germans plundered French resources and appropriated half of the public revenue so there was no money for the French. He did not want us to lose pride in our nation.

Papa would share the news, speaking to us as if we were adults; he didn't soften the details or filter descriptions. The Germans used any reason to take hostages. They rounded up French men and prisoners of war and used them as forced labor in the persecution of the Jews in the concentration camps. Many of them rebelled and were shot.

He told us about what happened with the children in England. They were massively affected but were more protected than the French. The UK authorities decided to evacuate two million children from their homes near the coastlines when they saw what was happening with the chaos of the French exodus. It was the biggest exodus since biblical times.

The English called it Operation Pied Piper. By early September 1940, just when we were coming from Mimizan to Paris, there were 1.9 million English children gathered at railroad stations, not knowing where they were going or if brothers and sisters would be kept together. There were children of all ages. These masses of English children were moved in three days.

In London alone there were sixteen hundred assembly points for children to gather. Some never made it anywhere. They accounted for one in ten of the deaths during the blitz of London 1940–41. Those who did leave were given a stamped postcard to send to their parents with their new address and location. Every child had a name tag pinned inside his or her shirt with an ID similar to the handmade ones Maman pinned on us. Papa explained that the English evacuation was not compulsory; many parents kept their children, and parents with money invariably made their own arrangements.

There is no doubt that social strata made an impact on how these children were evacuated. Although they endured dislocation and rationing, in exchange they received food and lodging, and they didn't experience the starvation problems we did in the French occupied zone. Papa said that our constant relocating was his way of protecting his children, like the English were protecting theirs.

When Papa would tell us these stories, Charlotte was always the first to ask questions, and he would answer in a somber tone. We were never too young to learn. These were our formative years, the time that defined each of us, created the largest mounds and divots in our mental landscape. Like glaciers in the Ice Age, the war eventually melted away, but its path changed everything. The people we were once destined to be had been left in Blendecques, and we were growing up in an avalanche of unpredictable time lapses.

May 1941 was the first anniversary of our departure from Blendecques. We had covered about eighteen hundred kilometers, over a thousand miles, to reach starvation and dejection. We didn't celebrate our first anniversary of the war. We didn't celebrate Elisabeth's birthday on May 15 as she turned eight years old, or Édith's birthday on May 24 when she turned three. Édith had been given a gift already; she was the only one who was young enough to be mostly unscathed by our surroundings. She was still innocent. She didn't have to listen to the horror stories Papa brought home.

That wasn't true for the rest of us. We knew we were starving. We knew others were suffering far more. The extent of that torment could not be dreamed up even in those nightmares that are born in the deepest, darkest corner of a child's mind. No mind could envisage what was really happening to those people, but that didn't stop ours from trying and waking us in sweats, causing us to cling to our bedmates in absolute horror.

Papa knew we wouldn't survive if we stayed in Paris much longer. We were, indeed, starving, but we knew not to complain. We had become aware that we probably would die. This awareness is often attributed to the loss of one's childhood. I would argue that before we knew we would die, we first learned how to survive, and that is equally deflowering. We began to believe death was waiting for us, the way little ones expect the bogeyman in their closet or under their bed, that unsettling, uninvited presence that entices the imagination and seeks to unify your greatest fears with reality.

All those weeks from March until June 1941, my parents scrambled and discussed every possibility to relocate. So, when an unexpected opening came, they seized it without hesitation.

# PART EIGHT

# 34

## SAINT-MALO

*B*efore the war began, Grandmother Houzet and her two spinster daughters had established themselves on the northern coast of Brittany, in the famous walled backwater fishing port of Saint-Malo, founded over two thousand years ago. With its medieval granite ramparts, château, and monastery, the commune of Saint-Malo felt extremely safe from an encroaching war, as it was away from any main roads and led to nowhere. The seafood, brought in daily by robust fishermen who competed with brazen sailors for dockage, was plentiful for a family of growing children who needed fresh food desperately. So when Grandmother Houzet located a small villa for rent and urged Papa to let us come, he released us to this safe harbor.

At nine o'clock on July 1, 1941, Maman boarded a train to accompany the six of us to Saint-Malo. We scrambled onto the wooden slat benches of a second-class car, feeling the freedom of an escapade. I was given a far corner seat by the window facing forward, and an empty paper bag, just in case. I kept my nose glued to the window, watching the miles of farmlands dotted with tiny villages fly by, steeples to the sky, cows and sheep grazing, so calm.

There was little friction from enemies along the way. Those railway lines, while in the occupied zone, were off the beaten path of war activities, hardly worth keeping under surveillance at this point. But it was a slow run. The train stopped at many stations along the way, loading and discharging cargo and passengers. Wagons were packed with people and every imaginable kind of luggage. We played a guessing game. How many real or cardboard suitcases, baskets, boxes, crates, animals, satchels, briefcases, backpacks?

Forging a path, pushing with bags in front of them, people could hardly manage to get to the exit doors. Boarding passengers blocked the steps, shoving their way into the cars. Redcaps were useless, and delays accrued. The train was alerted to stop for a convoy here, or a herd of cattle crossing tracks there. We crawled most of the way.

The trip, which normally would take about five hours, took us sixteen hours at an average speed of sixteen miles per hour. By then, the one toilet per wagon was a disgusting cubbyhole, and everyone had run out of food. Smelling like pigs, we arrived a day late, finding our Tante Suze waiting for us impatiently, distraught with dour news.

The very day of our trip, a German ordinance had been plastered all over town that no French citizen, except for those who were established residents, had any right to come and settle in Saint-Malo, even for a short vacation. To Maman, this was inconceivable. We were at our destination, starving and anxious to at least go to a bathroom, and there was Tante Suze, gabbing away with shifty gesticulations, telling us to head right back to Paris.

Obstinate and determined, as she could be under extreme duress, Maman hopped off the train, grouping us in tandem, dirty, malodorous, and famished, and demanded to be taken immediately to the villa, where she succumbed once more to an uncontrollable hemorrhage.

Tante Suze, flummoxed and distressed, repeated many times, "Elisabeth…but, Elisabeth…" but it was no use.

Maman lay there flat on the bed, having not even removed her shoes, eyes closed, refusing, probably unable, to budge. She waved her hand to shoo her aunt away, whispering, "*Demain, demain* (tomorrow)…"

Between her legs, a white towel was slowly blooming with red spots. No one was there to shoo me out, so I remained glued to the back wall, mesmerized, absorbing everything. Though I told myself this was no time to cry, I suddenly burst into tears and wailed at the horrible spectacle.

"Maman! Maman!" I cried hopelessly. Petrified, I felt the agony that she was going to die.

At this impasse, my brave oldest sister, Charlotte, stepped in and said, "Tante Suze, don't worry, I will go with you to talk to the Germans! But first let's go get the doctor. Maman is very ill."

Tante Suze was a finicky, phlegmatic old maid of icy disposition who talked down to her listener from the tip of her nose.

"Oh, no, that will not do!" she sniffed, avoiding any glance toward the sickbed and the blood. "The doctor does not take calls until after his nap, until four o'clock. It is really much more important to go see the *kommandant*, and he will get a doctor, but," she glanced at me, "not children. They cannot go with us."

Charlotte, fifteen years old and almost as tall as her aunt, had learned a bit of tact and *savoir-faire* with all the doctors and nurses around Maman in Paris. Now what she saw was a repressed, prissy woman in a tight black dress, wire-framed spectacles, and gray hair pulled back in a bun telling her no in so many words, but she refused to be intimidated. She looked up seriously, gave off a crinkly smile that shuttered her eyes and flaunted her perfect teeth, took her aunt's stiff hand by her side, and said, "Tante Suze, *allons-y!* (let's go)."

And off they went to see the Germans and request a doctor.

Their walk, from the train station to the city hall now harboring the German *kommandatur*, enchanted Charlotte in every detail. The old stone houses were pressed tight to each other in the narrow streets. Their small windows, each with its own green shutter held open by a big iron hook, would be closed as soon as a heady north wind came from La Manche. The old pockmarked front doors were hand-carved wood, each different, all up one step from the sidewalk to avoid flooding the front hall with frequent rains. Planters of red geraniums popped up everywhere, and lovely strips of gardens and vegetable patches could be seen behind small gates.

All these wonders put Charlotte in a good mood to convince her first listener, a young German in uniform, that there was no way Maman could possibly move out of her bed. She was sick, and she was dying.

There was blood all over. There were six of us, and we were starving, and we were filthy, and we smelled horrible.

Charlotte did not stop until given a promise that help would be available shortly. Tante Suze wouldn't show that she was impressed and stood by mute, still, locking hands all the way back to the villa.

Soon a very proper German officer arrived to check out the veracity of this breathless report given to his underling by a charming teenager. He couldn't believe it, but all of it was true, unlike many stories he heard from the natives wheedling for the slightest favors. Maman was really sick. It was obvious that we required help as he lined us up to count us, six starved and disgusting looking children. He sent over a doctor, provisions, a young housekeeper to clean up and cook, and gave us a *laissez-passer* for fifteen days.

Our enemy turned into our savior; we had a reprieve and we put it to work. The doctor not only helped Maman get well, but he also took her to see his good friend the mayor, a charming man who understood our predicament. They agreed that a stay in the vicinity would be extremely beneficial for all concerned, but a challenge to the decree could be dangerous. One simply did not cross the Germans, for fear of arrest for insubordination. They had their orders, and we had to comply.

Within the two weeks of salvation at the villa, the mayor accompanied Maman to meet the mother superior of a convent in Saint-Servan, only five kilometers down the coast. Mother Superior subsidized her convent by running an old-age pension in a wing of the monastery and assured Maman she would find room for us. Exacting a promise from her, stating that she could not afford to have her pensioners bothered by boisterous children, she demanded that we be quiet and attend church services every day.

Maman scoffed at the idea of us screaming, playing, or even laughing, a sound she had not heard for months. We were too sickly and depressed to do anything but survive. She promised everything and prayed that, with the help of Mother Superior, we would be moved to safety. In Saint-Servan, rules and decrees were different, and the Saint-Malo jurisdiction could not touch us. Much to Maman's relief, we were suddenly captives of the Catholic Church and protected by all the saints in heaven.

# 35

## SAINTS IN SAINT-SERVAN

*T*o the east of Brittany, the war raged on. Nazis firmly controlled the French occupied zone locked in by the demarcation line, resulting in much distress and starvation. They began their Operation Barbarosa to invade Russia, sending two hundred bombers for their first air attack on Moscow. Even worse, they developed their terrifying Final Solution. Hermann Goering signed the order drafted by Adolf Eichmann for the extermination of the Jews throughout Nazi-occupied Europe. Heinrich Himmler announced the development of a large-scale killing center at Auschwitz. Rudolf Höss was put in charge of its execution. And thus began the most ignoble part of World War II: the rounding up, incarceration, and extermination of millions of Jews throughout Europe. These men, these German *kommandants*, were only a few of the twenty-five thousand men finally responsible for this horror, and few have ever been brought to justice for their crimes.

President Franklin Delano Roosevelt could not sit still. While the United States was still neutral in the war effort, he strongly committed American efforts to aid Great Britain and France. In May 1941, he authorized the Lend-Lease Act, giving him the authority to sell or lease war goods to governments whose defenses he deemed vital to the security of the United States. In August, he would sign the Atlantic Charter with Churchill in Newfoundland, a statement, not a law, detailing the goals and aims of the Allied powers concerning the war and the postwar world.

It was July 15, 1941, and things were quite calm in Brittany. Saint-Servan, marked by the famous Solidor Tower built in the fourteenth century on the estuary of the Rance River, was not known for much else. Tucked into a convent on a cove formed by a small estuary, we were safe.

It was called Les Corbières, from the bird *corbie*, a raven, a crow, of which there were plenty. A nun in full habit met us at the door of the retirement wing of the convent. She led us through a long corridor and up three flights of stairs without ever slowing down. My brother and I could not take our eyes off her. She looked so different from normal people. We were entranced by her religious habit flowing loosely around her and little clicking noises that came from somewhere in her skirts.

At floor level she wore a pair of functional black leather shoes with a slightly elevated heel and rubber soles so the clicks could not come from there. Walking, she seemed to float going forward with no oscillating movements. There were yards of black fabric covering her entire body. She was topped by a white *cornette* circling her face, covered by a long sheer black veil down over her shoulders and her back. She walked steadily in front of us, ensconced inside the *cornette*, and we couldn't see her face even when she turned halfway around to make sure we were following her. It was only when she stopped and opened the door to a bedroom that she finally faced us.

A large silver cross with Jesus nailed to it hung on her chest from a black cord around her neck, and a huge rosary of brown wooden beads dangled from a similar black cord that pulled her garment together at the waist, clicking as she walked. Ah, the mystery of the clicks was solved.

She bowed slightly to Maman and waved her young, pale hand into the room. "Madame, I am Sister Regina," she said, "and this is one of your bedrooms. The other two are just next door. They are all the same. You can choose whichever you want." On these words her pale face evaporated down the hallway in a cloud of black rush and tiny clicks.

This was the most extraordinary person we'd ever seen. To discover the secrets hidden within this enveloping attire became a passion for Bernard and me. We'd spy on the nuns every chance we got. There were plenty of occasions to run into them but very few chances to ever see more than the outside shell of what they wore. Walking up the stairs, staying two steps below, would only show layers and layers of fabric, and an occasional glimpse of black stockings. The sturdy shoes reached to the anklebone and were laced up. Everything was black under there, from the floor up to the face, where the white *cornette* seemed to glow.

At first, all the nuns looked alike, some shorter and some taller, some with blue eyes some with brown, some with glasses some without. We could not distinguish one from the other just from a pale face and a pair of hands. Then as the days went by, little by little, we began to tell them apart. Sister Béatrice Anne-Marie was always smiling. Sister Gertrude Adeline was wrinkled, dry, and serious. Sister Mathilde Joseph would reveal the bon-vivant side of a chubette. Sister Irène Hélène seemed often surprised by her surroundings. Sister Thérèse Eugénie was extremely shy.

The life of a sister was a daily routine of work and prayer. We would encounter one or the other at a certain time in a certain place. They weren't allowed to converse with us except for saying *bonjour* and *bonsoir*, and we were much too shy to say more than, "*Bonjour, ma Sœur*" (Hello, Sister). They used their two large pockets down the side of their robes to carry handkerchiefs and little prayer books, which they would read while walking down the long hallways. Their sleeves were quite wide and would be turned up if they had to do a special job, revealing white starched cotton cuffs. We'd see them carrying baskets from the garden to the kitchen. They grew quite a lot of fresh vegetables, but we were not allowed to explore back there. We'd find the vegetables on our plates and would feel they were special because they came from right there, the fresh soil behind the building. We had asparagus, string beans, potatoes, carrots, beets, other root vegetables—quite an assortment, mostly boiled and served plain. We got used to the earthy taste of each one.

The laundry lines to hang the wash to dry in the sun were in the back of the convent, away from our retirement wing. Bernard and I tried to sneak a peek over there occasionally, always mystified to see white sheets and pillowcases clipped on the lines, but nothing personal. Why not their underwear? We knew there had to be some, somewhere.

All the time we lived there, the nuns remained quite inexplicable creatures, and I loved their untouchable enigmas. They were our saints: they hovered around but didn't touch us; they fed us, but we didn't see them cook; they took care of the old people, but we never saw how they did that. Everything worked like magic. It was quiet, it was beautiful, it was miraculous. We were in heaven with our own assembly of saints to watch over us. We were safe, we were fed, we slept well, we were angels.

# 3 6

## BENEDICTION

We were settled two to a bedroom and everything was bright and radiant in the summer sunshine. The furniture was white and glossy, a four-drawer dresser, a night table between twin iron beds, the thin mattress on a bouncy weave of springs, a chair and writing table, and transparent curtains that hovered around the window. We could leave the windows wide open, holding them in place with a large metal hook so they wouldn't bang and break against the thick stone walls on the outside or against the sill if slamming shut. Nothing would exasperate the adults more than if you left a window unhooked; it was a stern offense.

By climbing on a chair, I could just reach the metal oval handle and turn it clockwise to unlock the window. Then I would carefully push one side and put the big hook into a hole in the bar on the bottom of the frame, move my chair, and secure the other side. We could smell the fresh sea air day and night and could even see the harbor; our window was elevated above the rocky shore.

The sheets and bedspreads were plain and white, and we were taught how to make our own bed each morning. Straighten the bottom sheet, then pull the top sheet down, around the mattress, and up, and fold it over the blanket that covered it, fluff up the pillow this way and that, throw on the cotton bedspread so it would lie perfectly flat without bumps and folds. We had to pull it down for our naps and then pull it back up afterward. Édith was still too small to do this work, though she tried, and I helped her each day, as we shared a bedroom.

Zabeth and Fanny had another room. Charlotte and Maman were together. Bernard was put up somewhere else in a tiny room under the eaves. He loved being alone for the first time in his life. Everybody, young and old, shared the only two bathrooms down at the end of the hallway.

We devotedly went to the holy service every day. In church we were assigned a particular pew in the back. All the nuns filled up the six front rows, lined up five on each side of the aisle. They entered in a double file, led by the Mother Superior. Mother Raphaella was her name, but her status required that she be called Mother Superior.

Each nun looked respectfully down at the dark maroon tiled floor humming hymns, always the same ones. Then came all the pensioners, making muted geriatric noises as they shuffled into their pews and shuffled out and in again for Sunday communion, sometimes getting mixed up, forgetting where they were. All of us Gaillets entered last and filled up the back row, quiet as little church mice.

Regular as clockwork we went to eight o'clock Mass every morning, a low Mass with no sermon or hymns, which took all of thirty minutes from the first prayer to the final benediction. We would arrive five minutes early, dip our fingers into the holy water, make the sign of the cross, walk to our pew, genuflect on one knee in the center aisle, and file in to kneel at our designated place on a low padded hassock. Soon the priest would have us rise as he intoned the first prayer at the altar, and he would zip through the Mass in Latin, giving communion to the nuns only, and dismiss us with a blessing, "Go, Mass has been said."

Sunday nine o'clock High Mass was the most beautiful time of the week for me. We had to get dressed in the only good outfit we had: matching dresses for the four girls with handmade smocking across the front and a little half belt tied in the back. Underneath, only a pair of little white panties, a pair of small white cotton gloves on our hands, and white socks and black shiny Mary Janes on our feet.

Charlotte wore her usual white blouse with a navy skirt. My brother wore a pale gray suit that he was not growing out of, much to the despair of Maman, who could see that I was getting taller. We would get there early, and I'd fall into the magic of it all. I was entranced with the rhythm of the ritual, the nuns singing beautiful hymns I learned to hum, the golden bells ringing at the offertory when the host and chalice would rise above the head of the priest.

Everyone would bow down, incense burning, when the acolyte waved the ornate brass chain censer toward the congregation, first to his right, then to his left, then to the center, leaving little puffs of smoke to rise toward the apse. We were so far back in the chapel, the peculiar smell would take time to reach me, and I could predict the moment it would engulf me with its sanctity.

From the very first minute, I loved the familiarity of the entrance procession, always knowing exactly what was going to happen next, when to get up, to sit, to kneel, and to bow my head down and pray.

Maman and Charlotte alone would go up for communion; we were still too young and hadn't had catechism lessons yet. Together, the whole community would recite *Pater Noster, Credo,* and *Sanctus, Sanctus, Sanctus,* all in Latin that we learned by rote, just hearing it week after week. This repetition every Sunday brought us security and was the weekly anchor to our simple daily lives.

# 37
## REGIMENTED ADAPTATION

*I*n the retirement wing, the main floor, called *le rez-de-chaussée*, held three salons, a library, and the big dining room used by everyone except for the nuns, who had their own quarters that we never visited. They didn't eat with us because they served our meals. Except for an occasional glance into their mysterious lives, we had little notion as to when they ate, when they slept, what they did, and when they did it.

Then there were floors one, two, and three with all these similar bedrooms lined up on each side as in a hospital, and the fourth floor where Bernard had his tiny room. Old people reigned; we were the only children on the premises.

As a safety factor, the bedroom doors did not lock, dysfunctional keys having been misplaced for years. Above each door was a transom that opened and closed with a steel bar on the side, so you could ventilate the room without opening the door. The transom panel was made of mottled glass so we had the low hallway nightlight giving off a glow into our room. This nightlight guided us to the toilet, a separate cubbyhole from the bathrooms. That one had to be locked lest the pensioners would pull and bang on the door, needing to go right away.

Twelve noon for lunch, six o'clock for dinner, everybody ate at the same time in the huge dining room. We could hear the rumpus of loud voices of half-deaf people and the clatter of forks and knives on the plates. We could hear the slurp of soup spoons. At certain meal times,

181

sinewy food would be served, like artichokes, and there would be almost complete silence while the crowd sucked on the leaves, one at a time, careful of their dentures.

These old people smelled and coughed and snorted and talked to themselves. Many of the men smoked wherever they went, except for the dining room, where it was forbidden. They clicked their dentures and sometimes brought them in a water glass right to the dining-room table. We avoided them because of the way they'd stare and sneer. There was a mutual antipathy between us. Even if we were innocent, they complained we were impossible. We felt unjustly reprimanded and knew they were embittered by our presence. They thought it was preposterous that the nuns would put us up when there was so much room "elsewhere," meaning elsewhere in the world but not in "their" house. This was their home, and they had no place to go, but surely we little brats could be accommodated where we wouldn't be underfoot. Though we behaved quite responsibly and avoided them like anthrax, this wall of antipathy was never torn down.

Poor old things, they had obviously never been young at any time; the chasm between the generations was enormous. Maman didn't even bother to make friends while she was there. She spent all her time with us, or resting and reading. She was content to be with us in this constrained but serene environment.

During those two weeks at Saint-Malo, we had become a popular sight during our morning walks. From our rented villa to the seaport, from the fishing boats to city hall, to public parks, we had become the mascots of many residents, who quickly learned our routine and would come out on their front steps to see this unusual sight, and we continued the same parade in Saint-Servan.

Starting at ten after our hot chocolate and *tartine* with butter and jam, Maman would take us through the streets like a circus through town, marching us like toy soldiers. Maman would lead, her strength returning with the fresh sea air pumping into her lungs, radiant as always. With her hair in a well-kept French twist, and her feet shod in elevated cork sandals, she walked tall and proud. Wearing a printed summer dress with a sweater casually wrapped around her shoulders, she made it a point to take different streets, to point out an old church or a monument, to stop for a fishing boat docking, to wave back to people who waved at us. If the priest or some official-looking person passed by, she'd nod slightly and turn around to make sure we'd do the same. We would exaggerate a bow and giggle.

Édith was privileged to hold her hand because she was only three years old. She certainly was the cutest with her halo of curly blond hair and dimples in her cheeks. Bernard and I would be next, most likely holding hands. Zabeth and Fanny followed, one behind the other. We three girls were identical with bobbed hair and attire. Locals came out to witness and whispered how precious we looked in our navy-blue shorts with elastic waistband and slightly scratchy *pulls marins*. Our little brown sandals kicked up puffs of dirt on unpaved paths.

Charlotte, however, differed with curly hair, towering a head taller than Fanny. In her own clothes of a navy skirt and white blouse, she'd bring up the tail end. Her nose in the air in haughty indifference, trying to ignore us and look studious about architecture, she did her job as the caboose and brought the end of our little train safely to our destination. She was dreaming of returning to Paris.

# 38

## FEARS AND FEVERS

Living within the confines of a convent imposed a very different pace of life. Until that point, we had been taught decorum and perfect etiquette, but we now had to learn strictures and regulations of a dissimilar species. Lovely nuns flitted by in black habits, but we were not allowed to converse with them. Our building wing was full of seniors who could not bear the slightest deviation from their schedule, so we had to conform to it. We learned to anticipate consideration for people with canes, crutches, and wheelchairs. We learned a specific quality of silence: be silent, as in don't talk or giggle in the hallways, stay quiet in any part of the buildings, whisper but certainly not in church, keep doors from slamming, and God forbid, don't let an unhooked window slam! We learned to disappear. Silence was a demanding commandment, the hardest one to observe, the purest form of obedience.

There was a small beach down a little dirt trail to which we were taken with some regularity. This was wonderful, because it was not rocky like most of the Breton coastline but quite nice and sandy. It felt like decades since we'd been insouciant in Mimizan, and each trip was sheer ecstasy.

Our young local day-care person loved going into the water. She took delight in showing us how to swim. One day she carried me in her arms into water that came up to her shoulders. And then she threw me into deep water, laughing and saying, "Swim! Come on, swim!"

I was petrified! It was the first time I couldn't touch the bottom. I paddled and swallowed water, went under a couple of times as she watched me struggle, finally pulling me to her. Barely catching my breath, I screamed when she suddenly threw me out again to see if her instructions had any effect. After several of these submersions, she brought me back to the beach, and I ran away as far as I could from the water's edge. Angry and mortified, I wouldn't talk to her for days. It left a mark. It took courage to get over my fear of water as I grew older, but eventually I joined the swim and diving teams in high school.

One day on the way down the trail, Maman tripped and fell badly, cutting open her knee on a rock. Blood spurted out, terrifying me. I couldn't stop staring at the dark red flow running down her leg, dripping into the dirt the way those red spots had spread on the towel between her legs. She was so rarely with us and now in jeopardy. Would we lose her this time? Charlotte ran back up to get help, and the gardener arrived with some rags. His big brown boots caked with mud made her bare legs look ever so fragile. Like a pod of seals, we wailed and cried. Here was my unyielding Maman, sitting in the dirt, holding her leg with two hands, trembling, showing us that she was vulnerable. It would be my turn soon enough.

We often walked along the quays lined up with massive anchor bollards shaped like giant mushrooms, which the Germans used to erect coils and coils of barbed wires from one to the next, to fortify the area in anticipation of an attack. We were forbidden to go near them. But one day, dawdling behind the governess who was walking ahead with Édith and Bernard, I felt myself almost magnetically drawn to this iron mushroom, the top ever so slightly rounded, black, and shiny. For some inexplicable reason I felt that I must climb onto it. I knew it was forbidden, but I had to do it. "Just this one time," I thought as I put one slender foot on it and began to move my way up. I stood atop facing the beach, so proud, so free.

Turning to call to Bernard, my foot slipped on the downward curve. The somersault in my stomach happened just as my whole body twisted into a mangle of barbed wires. I screamed myself hoarse. I was lacerated from head to foot: my face, my neck, my naked arms, and through my clothes. The governess came rushing, beside herself with recriminations, scolding me loudly for my disobedience, scaring my poor brother and baby sister with her invectives, while I lay there helpless and petrified, bleeding like a pig.

It took three men over an hour to spring the wires and extricate me, causing further wounds. Wrapped in a blanket, doused in blood and tears, I was rushed to the hospital, where I was sedated and sewn up like a rag doll. I was hospitalized for three days for fear of infections from all the rust on the wires.

Delirious nightmares about death and disfigurement tormented me for weeks, blood intermingling from Maman and me, burial in the same hole in the ground with Bernard looking down and calling for someone to save us. The desperation of this little girl, not even six years old, was bottomless.

Soon after that, Elisabeth contracted a grievous case of typhoid fever. Maman believed she caught this bacterial infection, salmonella, on a visit to a nearby farm where she ate some food and drank water from a dirty glass in a filthy kitchen. As soon as it was diagnosed as very contagious typhoid fever, Zabeth was quarantined from everyone in a little room up on the fourth floor of our wing in the convent. Her door was kept closed at all times with a big sign on the doorknob: *Défense d'Entrer* (Do Not Enter). Her fever shot up to 104, she had uncontrollable diarrhea and vomiting, and there were no medicines available to cure her except for aspirin. Time was the tyrant that would decide her fate.

My godmother, Tante Thérèse, the young sister of Papa, was living in Marseille for the duration of the war. She heard about Zabeth and sent her a case of tangerines for its vitamin C.

Tangerines! We didn't even know what a tangerine was, and from my very own godmother, no less! Irrepressible curiosity led me up to the fourth floor unseen, creeping into her room, closing the door, and begging Zabeth for a tangerine. She was in the process of eating one right at that moment and without hesitation handed me half of it. I sat on the little chair and ate it. We talked. I told her my barbed wire scars didn't hurt so much though they striated my skin in bright red lines, a flag across my face, and she told me how sick she felt and how horrible it was to be away from all of us. After a while I sneaked back downstairs without telling anyone what I had done.

But my sin caught up with me that night. It began with cramps and vomiting, and the next day it became clear that I had typhoid fever. I had to confess that I'd gone to see Zabeth and shared a tangerine from my godmother. My poor mother was so upset she couldn't even punish me. She said the sickness was punishment enough and sighed while the nuns put up a cot between the far wall and Zabeth's bed. I lay there, gloom enveloping the saddest little girl on earth. Fortunately, the strain I contracted was milder than Zabeth's, and I began to recover while she continued to worsen.

# 39
## HOLOCAUST

*T*ime was moving toward the end of August 1941. For the past two months we had been cut off from news of the war. Living in a convent with nuns and old people, secluded in a tiny seaside village of mostly fishermen, it seemed like the war and the exodus we had experienced were just a bad dream. We thought we had managed to escape any more hardships. Nobody listened to the radio here.

The few Germans around town were complacent and sympathetic. We didn't have decrees and laws controlling our every step. I was recovering from my accident, and my scars were drying up and itching less. I also was convalescing from typhoid fever and so spent plenty of time lying there on my hard little cot, humiliated by my unexplainable behavior. There was nothing to do but to ask God for forgiveness, begging for His understanding. I was elated when I was allowed to return to Mass the last Sunday of August. And then, the biggest surprise came to cheer us up: Papa was coming to visit!

When Papa arrived for a few days, he reopened our wounds and fears. He did not believe in letting things go unspoken. "If you know a thing is wrong, you must share this feeling with others, lest you are as guilty for knowing and not saying," he said. It was during this visit that he told us about the horrific capture of Jews in mid-July.

Spreading out like locusts from villages to towns and cities, the Nazis located four thousand French Jews, who were arrested and taken into custody. Their children were abandoned in the streets, where neighbors who knew them, whose children played with theirs, were expressly forbidden to help them.

French Jews, foreign Jews, and anyone suspected of aiding Jews—no one was spared in this initial roundup. Men were separated from women and carted off to different holding locations, half-starved, deprived of proper sanitation, medical supplies, and food. Not a single soul whom the police could lay hands on was allowed to go free: not hospital patients, not mental defectives in asylums, not even the solitary families living in the backwoods. They rounded up everyone.

Over five thousand abandoned children were herded into school buildings, the little ones not even knowing their own names. Many died there before the survivors were shipped off to camps. Some escaped the roundups and were smuggled to safety, in spite of the danger involved for those who tried to help. We were so blessed to be Catholics in a Catholic convent during these times. But hearing Papa's stories petrified us. What was a Jew? What was a Catholic? How could they tell? Would we be picked up too by these frightening Nazis in bile-green uniforms and transported to a hell beyond comprehension?

And then, without warning, Papa, Maman, and Charlotte were gone!

Papa, Maman, and Charlotte, all three of them vanished from our lives. Maman took a train alone back to Paris. Papa and Charlotte left on their bicycles to ride the 250 miles home, in any kind of weather, with their papers in order, tucked deep in a pocket. Each had a small backpack with food prepared by the kitchen nuns; they knew they wouldn't find anything along the way in the occupied zone.

But in less than half a day, Charlotte felt ill and couldn't continue. She didn't have the stamina Papa did, the ability to pedal all day on every kind of road, not all of them flat. They reached a small railroad station and waited for a train. They knew there would be one sometime because people were waiting there patiently, sitting on their poor suitcases of ersatz leather and worn fabrics, held together with strings and cords. When a train finally arrived already crammed with passengers, they threw their bikes into the baggage car. They managed to get on only by climbing head first through a window into a wagon full of passengers.

We five children stayed in Saint-Servan until September 1942. For a full year, so long and yet so safe, we stayed peacefully, respectfully, and most of all silently in this monastery, at the mercy of the beautiful black-robed nuns, the grumbling old ones, and the young governess who didn't know how to teach us to swim. Alone together, we thrived. Maman came to visit a few times, and even stayed with us for the month of August 1942, but her visits remain unmemorable because they were so short, except for the last one, in mid-September, for Bernard's birthday. He would be eight years old, safely surrounded with caring sisters older and younger.

# PART NINE

# 40
## DEMARCATION LINE

The demarcation line clearly cut France into two uneven pieces. It was established on June 22, 1940, when Pétain accepted the total collapse and defeat of the French army and signed an armistice with the Germans.

Général de Gaulle, who had been the government leader until then, left immediately for London. He urged his countrymen to resist, giving birth to the Free French movement to keep the French dream alive in those grim days. On the BBC, de Gaulle refuted Pétain's capitulation to the Nazis and gave his famous appeal to continue to fight for France. "Whatever happens," he said, "the flame of the French resistance must not go out and will not be extinguished."

Unfortunately, de Gaulle was faraway, and Pétain was in Vichy, collaborating with the Germans. To the north, three-fifths of the country were occupied by the enemy. The Germans now blocked the passage of any person trying to go one way or the other over this line, the demarcation line. This was not a line with simple signs saying "Free Zone" on one side and "Occupied Zone" on the other. The demarcation line was a massive physical obstacle course, which ran for 745 miles from the Spanish border through Southwest France to the Swiss border north of Geneva. It was impregnable, massive, and dangerous.

The effect of the demarcation line was exacerbated by additional restrictions quickly imposed by the Nazis in outlying areas, insuring total control by their army. The southwest corner by Spain guaranteed them access into that country. They created the Atlantic Wall, a wide zone from land out to sea, along the entire French shoreline from Spain to Belgium, giving them access to the Atlantic Ocean. The only people allowed to enter the occupied zone were residents who had lived there at least three months and those who worked for the German army. No telegraphs or telephones were permitted. In the North and Pas de Calais, where we came from, the Nazis took control of thousands of acres rich in agriculture and industry, leaving little if anything for the French.

The forced-labor workers building the demarcation line arbitrarily chopped up roads, properties, villages, fields, gardens, woods, and any land or building in their way. At the will of the Germans, who placed an array of physical encumbrances to make it impossible to penetrate, forced-labor crews blocked all passages with barriers, barbed wires, huts, gates, and motley obstacles.

To control crossings, they placed numerous checkpoints staffed with soldiers: French on the free south side and Germans on the occupied north side. They made sure to stop every person and ask, "Are your papers in order?"

It was *infranchissable,* no one could go over it without a *laissez-passer;* it was *incontournable,* no one could go around it because hundreds of kilometers of obstructions completely blocked passage. Those returning home on the orders of the Germans found these obstacles impassable, and many were forced to find refuge where there was none, or resorted to bribes, fraud, and lies to get through. Cars loaded with families and baggage were subject to severe examinations, being ordered to open up everything, luggage, trunks, handbags: everything.

It was a chaotic debacle without precedent. Some German soldiers used their power to demand money for any little favor: 200 francs to deliver a letter or a package to someone nearby, then 500, and eventually 1,000 to 5,000 francs. There was no limit to their extortion.

As soon as night fell, the checkpoints suddenly closed. Lines of cars and pedestrians were forced to wait overnight. People openly used the side of the road to relieve themselves. They slept in a field on a blanket, or in a car sitting up. Food was scarce and hard to find if you didn't keep some in your vehicle. Even the hardy French lost their ability to adapt. They would try to convince a guard that their parent was home deathly ill or that someone had died, anything to cross over. But it was mostly hopeless, for they would be subjected to endless absurd questions and paperwork that kept them riveted in place. Once the line was established, strict controls quickly multiplied, and by spring of 1941, it was off to jail or even death for trying to force through.

Then there were clandestine groups, underground volunteers who took on dangerous activities. They tried to help escaped French prisoners or conscripts from border cities that refused to join the German army and needed to reach the free zone. Numerous men and women helped out because they hated this enemy hacking their country in two. They took their lives in their hands every minute they exposed themselves to danger. The example of their heroism was contagious. As long as they survived, they worked endlessly. Sometimes they would be caught and shot on the spot. They were true heroes.

This, however, made life extremely dangerous for those who were legally entitled to cross the line. There were regular citizens like Papa who ran a legitimate business, a business from which he tried to stave off Nazi Germany. He was forced to go back and forth with a *laissez-passer*, the special government document to let him pass either way. Every time Papa was called to go to Vichy, which forced him across the demarcation line, he feared for his life, and yet he went. He had no choice.

He crossed and recrossed that line more than a dozen times, and each time it would be worse. He was never immune to the fear that grew in him, like an impenetrable nightmare, while waiting for his turn at the checkpoint. The soldiers were demanding and intimidating every time. He knew his papers were in order but he worried they might have something wrong he didn't know about as they were checked and rechecked. He thought his Rosengart would be requisitioned as it was subjected to dogged searches.

Papa was surrounded with families trying to get through, children crying, emaciated youngsters begging for food, women in rags, men desperate for some kind of help. Once, Papa was sitting in line, one car behind the checkpoint. "At last," he thought, "I can get out of here."

The car in front of him was being shark-attacked by German soldiers and French police. Angry voices howled into the car full of children. Papa could tell from the commotion that this wasn't an ordinary inspection.

"Out! Out of the car! Everyone, now!" a deafening voice screamed in German.

The driver, a middle-aged man with tattered clothes and tousled hair, began pleading in French.

"*S'il vous plaît*, I beg you, my mother is dying! There's no need for—"

He was abruptly silenced by the butt of a Nazi rifle across his face, blood fanning out from his nose, while a woman and three children crawled out of the car, screaming.

Papa sat frozen, unable to believe this crime was happening. Had this not been a war and his life not in jeopardy, he would have intervened. But this was war, and the fact that he couldn't do anything was unbearable. He just had to sit and watch this barbarism, his hands clutching the steering wheel tighter. Two German soldiers were ripping the man's clothes off him, his family kneeling on the gravel in tears.

"*Jude!*" a German voice bellowed.

Papa's eyes widened, and his stomach curled like burnt paper. They were Jews. The two soldiers stood the man up against the car; naked, soaked in his own blood, and piss slithering down his thighs. Papa grated his teeth as he heard loud shouting and laughter.

Suddenly, one of the soldiers pulled out a Luger, put it to the man's temple, and pulled the trigger. The blow of the bullet sent the man stumbling a few feet back toward Papa's car. He sat in horror and watched the man die, blood percolating from the bullet wound, the man's eyes locked in permanent shock.

A stutter of machine guns started firing into the thickets off the roadside, aiming for the man's family in their attempt to flee. Papa sat paralyzed as he saw two of the three children hit from behind, falling like scarecrows in red plumes.

Papa sat there, livid and traumatized, as the soldiers and French police pushed the Jewish family's car off into the ditch to allow passage. He knew he was legitimate and that he had to feign pleasantries lest they subject him to similar scrutiny.

An officer waved him forward. His brain went into autopilot. He heard a French voice ask him if his papers were in order. Papa nodded, showed them the appropriate documents, and was cleared to pass. Five miles further he pulled over, shaking uncontrollably. He had to throw himself from the vehicle and vomit. He got back in the car and cried, wailed as he hadn't done since infancy. He closed his eyes and screamed out prayers to God.

# 41

## BERLIN BUSINESS

*I*n 1941, Papa had been obligated to go to Berlin to attend a meeting with the German controllers who oversaw the paper industry. He was offered a sleeping car on the Mitropa. The name is a derivative of Mitteleuropa, a German railway company founded in World War I as a first-class catering service managing railway sleeping and dining cars, which were extremely expensive and exclusive. The elegantly decorated carriages were a distinctive burgundy-red and sported a gold logo on the outside of each car. At either end were two closet-size spaces that normally served as resting quarters for the conductors but were now occupied by Papa's two escorts.

Papa knew one of them well, Lieutenant Hafner, who spoke a polished French without any accent and was enjoying his mission, both in the offices in Paris and now on the train to visit his homeland. Unfortunately, he later married a Swiss woman, a double crime against his homeland: first, mixed marriages weakened the German race, but even worse, the second crime was against German women; over a million never found husbands after 3.9 million German soldiers were killed during the war. As punishment, Hafner was sent to the Russian front, from which he never returned.

In Berlin, where the nightly activity and lights contrasted with dreary Paris, Papa and his representatives were received like royalty. They had a suite at the five-star Hotel Adlon by the Brandenburg Gate, furnished with magnificent antiques and sporting a sumptuous marble bathroom.

They were feted at the Hausbacher Restaurant, where he had the best dinner in months.

They were taken sightseeing and found the city still intact, showing not a single sign of war. Wilhelm Bracht personally guided them through the Aschaffenburg paper mills that were impressively modern and clean. Their plants far surpassed some of our old Avot-Vallée paper mills, which Papa promised himself to modernize at the first opportunity. He knew most of the ten men on the trip who, like him, had official functions during the war, *laissez-passers*, legal papers, and documents that allowed them to move between occupied and free zones and into Germany itself, trips he did not relish.

By inviting them to Berlin, the Germans wanted to set up the first steps of a major project whereby they intended to take control of all European purchases of cellulose pulp. They figured this would limit the speculation caused by the competition of buyers of different countries. Already, before the war, the English and French had agreed not to outbid each other, but this agreement had been undermined by the invasion of France. The Swedes, on the other hand, were neutral and refused to submit themselves to such an agreement, and Papa was in no position to try to convince them.

In 1943, the Svenska Cellulosa Aktiebolaget (Swedish Organization of Cellulose) asked Papa to consult with them about this situation in Stockholm and the position of France with Germany. They obtained a visa for him, allowing him to go to Sweden, but he had to once again travel to Berlin to pick up official papers. The contrast of that trip two years after the one in 1941 was shocking.

During the train ride through Saxony, he was transfixed by mile upon mile of factories, industries, and railroad yards lining the tracks, highly camouflaged so as to blend in with forests and fields. Berlin was now as dark as Paris. Many buildings had been bombed, their ruins partially hidden by large panels plastered with multicolored patriotic posters. He spent only one night at the deserted Hotel Adlon and, with new papers in order, caught an early train that ended at the beautiful little port of Sassnitz on the Baltic.

His lunch in the dining car revealed that German restrictions were becoming serious. Following an enormous platter of potatoes with onions came another, no less abundant, platter of white beans. Filled with starches, he came back to his compartment and met an old acquaintance, Gosta Hall, director of the Swedish pulp mills Stora Kopparsberg, who was returning from a trip to Italy. Hall was a very friendly and cheerful fellow.

"What!" he said. "You had lunch in the dining car? But that's a crime! The food is superb on board the ferry; most boats are run by Swedes." As the train slowed down for a skillful descent through cliffs to water level, Hall declared triumphantly, "What luck! It is the Swedish ferry!"

Passenger control was nominal and at the precise moment the last dock line was free, the restaurant bell rang, and everyone rushed to the bar. Incapable of resisting the temptation of a smorgasbord, washed down with aquavit and followed by exquisite lamb chops, Papa felt guilt at his gluttony, which was somewhat assuaged by the thought that it wouldn't last. After a five-hour crossing, they docked in Tralleborg, at the southern tip of Sweden.

Those five days he spent in Sweden were an enchantment. He had forgotten what life was like for people at peace, without real worries. Papa spent a good part of the first night on his balcony at the Grand Hotel, viewing the luminous display of advertisements of all colors, which lit on and off to promote the qualities of some of the products he most missed in France. All these scintillating lights were mirrored in the waters of the canals like so many stars. He was captivated and had a hard time falling asleep, thinking about his lovely wife.

When he went through Berlin again some months later, a new series of English bombardments had caused terrible damage. There was no question anymore of hiding the destroyed buildings with publicity panels. The Hotel Adlon had disappeared. Gosta Hall told Papa later that he had unfortunately left two suitcases in their storeroom, as he stayed there often. They both stayed at the nearby Bristol Hotel but had to spend part of the night in the basement bar, which had been transformed into a shelter. The fortunes of war were turning.

# 42

## PARIS ART GALLERY

*At 3 Rue des Saints Pères on the Left Bank, Maman became a renowned art dealer during and after the war. She was heartbroken when she had to sell the gallery in 1946 when we moved to Larchmont, New York.*

*A*t the end of summer 1941, having left us in Brittany under the kind auspices of the Mother Superior and her flock of devoted nuns, my parents continued to live in occupied Paris in du Plessix's grandiose apartment on the third floor of 6 Rue de Longchamps, facing the quiet sloping street in the front and the busy courtyard in the back.

Maids and cooks would dump their garbage in dark gray bins and take time out to chat, their voices echoing around the walls past the sixth floor up to the clouds. Rubbing their chafed hands on rough cotton aprons, they complained about everything, compared notes about their employers, commiserated about their own families faraway in the country, and then went back to their jobs.

Free of children or housekeeping responsibilities since Arthur and Léontine took care of everything, my parents enjoyed a lot less pressure and even some measure of quality of life. While still complicated, provisioning requirements were minimal for just the four of them and so much easier in this quartier. Whatever came on the table satisfied them easily.

Often they rode their bikes over to see Bon Papa at Rue de la Trémoille, where Hortense surpassed herself in turning bland ingredients into delicious concoctions. Balancing leftovers on handlebars, my parents returned home quickly by the small streets before curfew.

Nonetheless, Maman was miserable knowing that to avoid a repeat performance of the terrible winter of 1940, her children had to stay put. Only thirty-seven years old, Maman began to think she should acquire some kind of occupation. Paris was at half-mast yet safe in so many ways that there must be some work she would find fulfilling. She had learned much running the show in Mimizan; surely there was someone, something, where she could apply her savoir-faire to some benefit. With many empty days and nights she grew restless, especially as Papa was away on business much of the time. When he was there, she was as impassioned as she had been in the first days of their marriage; the strength of their love was so profound, it couldn't be plumbed or punctured.

On weekends when Paris was somnolent and Papa wasn't working, they whipped around on bicycles in the deserted city, which was practically free of motorized traffic. They loved ferreting through semidark antique shops and art galleries on the Left Bank. Wobbling on their bikes around the small cobbled streets of the old *quartiers* one Saturday, they stumbled on a sign *A Vendre* (For Sale) posted discreetly in the bottom corner of the window of a small gallery. They stopped and, hands cupped on the window to shield the glare, they saw misshapen piles of artworks strewn around a somewhat dilapidated shop. Stepping back, looking up through years of dirt, they saw a dark green sign with gold lettering: Galerie André, 3 Rue des Saints Pères. They looked at each other, entered the gloomy space, and unknowingly changed the course of their lives.

The weary proprietor showed signs of frustration as he described his situation. His story was no different from many others. His mistress had been in charge, but she had died a few months back. He was leery of hiring anyone new. He still went to a boring day job as a bank clerk on weekdays, so he could open only on Saturdays.

Maman started to daydream.

This man confided to my parents that he would gladly sell the gallery and retire if he could only find a buyer. He talked about the stock he had accumulated for the past thirty years. More than three thousand drawings, etchings, prints, and lithographs were asleep in cardboard portfolios, with prices that seemed ridiculously low. There were piles of these resting against the walls, on tables, on the desk, in the back room, haphazardly placed in such a way as to make it impossible to even sell one if he wanted to. In other words, the place was a shambles and needed an entire makeover.

Maman's excitement grew as they began to look through some of the pictures. There was artwork of every kind, from the worst to the best.

"Who would be interested in this kind of business at a time like this?" he complained.

His question hit her like a lightning bolt. It was her eureka moment, and from that day on, she could talk about nothing else. She was convinced that this forlorn art gallery was the perfect remedy to pull her out of her loneliness, and she made it clear to Papa that she would use her own money to acquire it.

The following Saturday morning, on their bikes from Rue de Longchamps to Rue des Saints Pères, through the Trocadéro, along the Right Bank of the Seine, flying over the Pont des Arts, my parents covered the two miles in record time, fueled by resolution. Breathless and flushed, they sat down with the owner to get more details and to inquire about his terms.

The owner was taken by surprise. He never expected to see that eager young couple again. He never even asked why my parents were interested, or what background in art had led them to want his gallery. Making a fast deal was foremost on his mind. He presented an irresistible bargain with very reasonable terms. He was anxious to retire. He needed only a little capital to help cushion his bachelor lifestyle, unencumbered by family or children. He wanted 100,000 francs for the business, including the lease transfer, and 50,000 for his stock.

Ever the wary executive, Papa had reservations about the value of the stock, which looked like a mess, even though the asking price was ridiculously low. He rummaged through some of it again and agreed to buy the whole lot at 40 percent off the list price. To his surprise, this turned out to be quite a bit more than the original asking price but, without haggling, he paid the required sum of 400,000 francs ($4,000 at the time).

Maman was ecstatic when they signed the deal. Right in the middle of the war she became the proud owner of an art gallery a few steps from the Seine, on the Left Bank of Paris, an inconceivable dream.

Maman couldn't believe her luck. Her mind veered quickly from somber news of the war and worries about the children, which were always tormenting her, and turned her focus to her gallery. She quickly hired a couple of day workers from the neighborhood and, with an innate sense of creativity, gave the place a modern, clean, and stylish look. Having never signed a check in her life, and with not the slightest notion of accounting, she went headlong into the ownership of a business and, somehow, succeeded brilliantly.

Her first working tool was an eraser. She carefully removed prices marked on works of art and increased them appreciably. Without revealing her new calling, she found out what their current values might be by visiting other galleries. She said that often she didn't even erase a number but would just add a zero at the end, or even two. She had a genius for switching from etchings and lithographs to paintings and aquarelles, discovering young painters and changing her exhibitions often so she could expect a bigger turnover.

At 10 Avenue de Messine, in the prestigious eighth arrondissement, was a renowned dealer, Louis Carré, who had founded a first-class gallery in 1938. Known for representing and exhibiting modern masters—Gris, Klee, Matisse, Calder, Léger, Delaunay, Kupka, and Picasso—Carré also showed the works of Jean Bazaine, Maurice Estève, Charles Lapicque, and Jacques Villon, lesser known artists at the time. He was considered one of the great Parisian art dealers. Papa knew him well from handling difficult requests for deliveries of special papers.

Just a few months earlier, Carré wanted to print a limited edition of lithographs by Raoul Dufy on rare and hard-to-get art paper that Papa had been able to procure. As a way of thanking him, Carré offered to put Maman in touch with promising painters who did not yet deserve their consecration with an exhibit in his own gallery. She launched a few, while making her own discoveries: Dubuffet, who was to become very famous, Jean Dufy, the brother of Raoul, whose following was growing steadily, and several others. These artists became the beacon that brought fame to the Galerie André before long.

In those days, some Parisians had quite a bit of disposable money but had trouble finding safe ways to spend it. In a time of war, spending on luxuries was highly distasteful and suspect. Artworks and jewelry were considered safe private investments. If you had the means to find food first, often on the black market that was thriving behind the back of the Germans, then you could luxuriate in an oil painting or a diamond bracelet and keep them hidden easily. Maman was an expert at keeping secrets and, being a dealer, had every right to strap a painting to her bicycle to drop it off "somewhere," no questions asked. Her books showed sales to names like Smith, Brown, and Jones.

In the back of the gallery, beyond the ground-floor space open to the public, was a little office leading to a toilet and, beyond, a closed door. A tiny stairwell behind this door led six steps up to a small loft and bath, with only one window on the courtyard, therefore very dark. Maman fixed it up very simply with a desk, a chair, an armchair, a swing-arm lamp for both, a single bed, and, to break up the monotony, a colorful Moroccan rug. Except for the rug, it was just like a monastery room. Her intention was to be able to sleep there should she work too late to ride her bike home after curfew and to save time commuting back and forth when Papa was away.

But this room wasn't to be her cocoon of safety. One day soon after she opened her doors, a tall, stooped, skinny man walked in with some paintings under his arm. He was dejected and tattered, and he looked gaunt and desperate.

"Madame," he said, "help me. Please…"

Moving him away from the front door toward the back of the gallery, she let him line up his paintings against the wall, while he said, "I will give you these…" His voice quavered, and his eyes were alarmed and weary like a frightened animal. Maman was at once repelled and touched by his condition while very attracted to his art.

"And your name is?"

"Non, I don't have a name anymore. I have no family." He trailed off.

"Are you hungry?" Maman asked maternally. The haggard young man paused for a moment then quickly nodded, his head down, looking at the floor.

"Please sit down," Maman said softly, pointing to the back office. The young man hesitated, his eyes darting back and forth in fear and suspicion.

He finally lifted his head up and looked at Maman.

"It's OK. You're safe here. You can trust me," she said. The young artist finally followed her back to the office. He winced when Maman turned on the light. She turned it off with a sigh.

"Perhaps it's best to keep the light off. Eyes are everywhere these days," Maman said and nodded to the desk chair. He slowly sat down, heaving a sigh of relief as if he'd been standing for years.

"I'll be right back," she said, walking to the front of the gallery, drawing the nightshades, and locking the doors. She hesitated, it was still early, someone might question her closing at this time, but then she firmly flipped the sign to read *FERMÉ* on the street side and glided back to her unexpected guest. She quickly sliced some bread and a small wedge of cheese, adding half a tomato. She walked the small plate back to him.

"It's not much, but—" she began to say when the young man quickly grabbed it and began to devour the food ravenously, licking it from his soot-stained fingers.

"Merci, ah, merci Madame," he repeated, muffled by mouthfuls of bread and cheese. The sight of him so helpless strengthened Maman's resolve to help him.

She learned he was a Polish Jew on the run from the army and from the Gestapo, a target for raids by German soldiers and French police. She asked again, but he wouldn't give her his name. He said it was too dangerous; he had lost track of his family. She feared the repercussions that could befall our family if she helped him; she could be shot on the spot if discovered. She knew she should just give him some money for the paintings and let him out in the street. She had relatives who were prisoners of war at that very moment and thought of them. He looked so forlorn and lonely, her mind whirling with apprehensions, but eventually her decision was made, though it went against the tide of safety.

All his answers to her questions were no. No food, no room, no money, no relatives, no one. He was truly a fugitive with nothing. She gave him some money for the paintings, which she deemed were quite good, and in an act of folly and faith, she also offered him the studio as a hidden shelter. He moved in with not much more than what he was wearing on his back and slept for hours that first day. She told me much later how his presence elated and scared her to the same degree, like having an illicit affair. But once embarked on saving him, she could never change her mind.

Little by little, her life took on an unusual rhythm of exhilaration and anxiety. Strict rules were set for his safety. She showed him an emergency exit through the courtyard and instructed him, "You must never go out in the street. If you smoke, blow it out the window but keep the shade down so people around the courtyard can't see you from their windows. Don't smoke when there are servants in the courtyard, they would notice right away and set off an alarm thinking it might be a fire. If you need something, you must write a note and slip it out under the door. You must never come out unless I knock on the door." They established a knock-knock code. He spoke good French, and that was helpful. He readily agreed to all her conditions; with her he felt safe for the first time in months.

Maman's exhilaration at saving a life was tremendous, but her anxiety intensified. She was hiding a Jew from both the Germans and her husband, who she knew would harshly reprove her. She snitched some cigarettes from Papa, as they were found only on the black market and sold only to men. She brought food to the artist that he would consume cold and return the plate immaculate, as if he had licked off every last crumb. She scoured the occasional church jumble sale for a sweater, a shirt, underwear, a pair of pants, to make him more comfortable.

Thus she fell into an unusual pattern of running the gallery up front, dealing with her artists, new friends, and visitors, making sales, going to openings, becoming a successful Parisian art dealer, and, on the darker side, making sure her fugitive was alive, comfortable, entertained with newspapers and magazines while patiently waiting for deliverance.

This fragile relationship held steady for almost a year, from the fall of 1941 to July 1942, without any mishaps. This was a miracle, considering his close quarters, her multitude of activities, and raids for Jews in every corner of the city. No one ever denounced him, because no one ever knew of his existence.

While Papa worked hard at the office, he was relieved that Maman thrived at Galerie André, until the day he found her filching cigarettes, and she confessed about the perilous arrangement with the painter. He was infuriated about her dangerous position. How she ever got the nerve to hide a Polish Jewish painter escaping from the claws of the Nazis he'd never know. The thought of how she wavered for months before telling him enraged him. Years later, Papa admitted that part of him always knew that Maman had more courage and heart than he would ever know. But then, faced with a *fait accompli*, he had to accept the poor man's presence, while his concerns about the situation kept him from ever broaching the subject.

Papa simply refused to talk about him, fearing the echo of his voice might carry to the nearest Nazi, who would arrest them. It was impossible to think of the consequences that would have befallen Maman, the family, their children, should she have been caught by a patrol canvassing the streets. Papa would describe the situation later with disdain draped in much love and pride for Maman's bravery. He said she had a beauty of spirit and a certain presence of character that he could not transcend, but it always seemed to protect her.

Without warning, this precarious balance was shattered one day in July, when the artist was attracted by an advertisement in one of the old newspapers scattered on his floor. Men's shoes were on sale at a very advantageous price only a few blocks away. The money from selling his paintings was burning in his pocket, and cramps were hurting his feet. These shoes had to be his. Exactly in the way I had been drawn to that mushroom bollard, he couldn't help himself. He stared and stared at those shoes in print and eventually succumbed to their appeal.

Maman had not arrived yet that morning. He broke the rules. He left through the emergency exit and, quickly crossing the courtyard, turned south down the street toward Boulevard St. Germain. His collar turned up, his hat down on his face, he tried to make himself invisible. But transparency is intangible; just like magic, it disappears.

His tall, lanky body was visible to anyone nearby. His luck turned when a French police patrol, always on the lookout for fugitives, stopped him.

"Are your papers in order?" they asked.

He could not show any papers and was arrested. He had gone out just when raids were more intense than usual that July, as there was a quota to fill for arresting Jews. Nazis strictly supervised the French police in various districts of Paris, during which more than four thousand stateless and foreign Jews were arrested that month. Even more devastating was the fact that he was reading an old newspaper. Had he had a more current issue, he would have known about the intensified raids and certainly would have stayed in his hideout.

Somehow Maman got word he was being held in the internment camp of Drancy, in a northeastern suburb of Paris. Built by the government in the late 1930s, this camp of dreadful high-rise residential apartment buildings was poetically called the "Silent City." The Germans had requisitioned it in 1940, thrown out all the residents, mostly poor blue-collar workers, and set it up as a detention center to hold "undesirables" until their deportation. Without Papa's knowledge, again, Maman took the grave risk of going on her bicycle to bring the artist some care packages—not just once, but twice. Soon he was deported to Auschwitz and was never heard from again.

Maman was lucky and blessed to avoid any kind of retribution from the police. The artist never denounced her and, bit by bit, with gloom in her heart, she erased all traces of his existence, keeping only one of his paintings for herself. On the order of Papa, unimaginably upset at her for placing the safety of a stranger over the family, she followed the trend of all Paris and closed down the gallery to come to Saint-Servan for the month of August.

By September the whole thing had blown over. Keeping his memory in her heart, Maman carried on as if this interlude had never happened.

The Galerie André was for her an excellent occupation, a full-time job, a fascinating learning curve, and the center of her life while we children were under safe care elsewhere. With a very low overhead, she brought in an excellent increase in revenue for the household. A year later, at the end of 1943, she was proud to prove to Papa, statements in hand, that her profits had that year surpassed his income.

They sold the gallery after the war for 3.5 million francs to a Madame Ducret, who knew nothing about art and shortly had to let it go to an expert, who soon restored its reputation under the name of Galerie Framont. That storefront has retained its clean-cut prewar appearance that, with an occasional coat of paint, looks exactly as it did when Maman owned it.

# PART TEN

# 43
## RUPTURE

On September 16, 1942, my brother Bernard turned eight years old, but he was only *almost* as tall as I was. Maman arrived in Saint-Servan to celebrate her one and only son's birthday. She had spent the month of August with us after the tragedy of her Jewish boarder, but she felt compelled to come for this very special birthday, the first birthday we would celebrate since 1939. Our childish handmade gifts were waiting, wrapped in newspapers and hidden under my pillow. But when Maman arrived, she had nothing but bad news.

On the train from Paris, she had run into the Mayor Delatour of Saint-Malo, who had been so helpful to us in 1941. Delatour was surprised to learn that we children were still in the convent, thinking we had been moved to the free zone months earlier. Maman reassured him that each time she visited, she found us well adjusted and growing in wisdom and age.

But Delatour had little patience for Maman's charming manners and begged her to listen carefully. He explained that the attack on Dieppe a month earlier had been devastating. Over six thousand men had been rebuffed at sea with a great loss of lives, an omen of much worse to come. The Germans were actively building the Atlantic Wall under our feet around Brittany to prevent the Allied Forces from landing on the shores of France and Belgium. This wall was impregnable. Thousands of forced laborers, abducted from Nazi-occupied countries, were constructing these permanent fortifications along the English Channel. Many of them died as a result of abominable living conditions, mistreatment, malnutrition, and disease. They were immediately replaced by other poor souls.

Delatour kept a close watch on war movements. He had no doubt that an evacuation of his district would happen soon. We had to go, he insisted, we had to leave immediately. He was in a near panic; his hometown was in great danger. Maman could not afford to be obstinate and leave us here. Completely devastated by the notion of bringing her children back to sure famine in Paris, she forgot Bernard's birthday altogether. She could only focus on what was, once again, the need for an immediate departure, and at the same time she couldn't help worrying about how this would affect her gallery.

I picked up our little packages from under my pillow and slipped them to Bernard, and we both cried. We had to say good-bye to Saint-Servan and the beautiful nuns, quiet and passive in the occupied zone. Within forty-eight hours our bags were packed, rooms were cleaned, farewells were said, and tears were shed by all of us. Sister Mathilde Joseph, who enjoyed an occasional foray off campus running errands for the convent, was in tears as she drove us in the convent's dilapidated van to the railroad station.

These stations in the occupied zone were always crowded with hundreds of people carrying all varieties of baggage, their children underfoot. Very few dogs or pets were seen by now. Trains were the only means of transport, as gasoline rationing made driving impossible. Getting us all together into a second-class car was a struggle, but Maman's authority and beauty did the trick. She towered over most of the people in her slightly elevated cork sandals and spoke kindly but firmly, so people moved to let us all in a compartment together, already filled with a crowd compacted on wood benches. When we arrived at Gare de l'Ouest, we could hardly believe that Arthur was there waiting for us. It was an overwhelming joy to be reunited.

However, by then Paris was in absolute agony, and my parents were desperate to find another location for us. Our return was like a monster that suddenly demolishes everything, and they couldn't handle it. We couldn't go to our church and pray; all the churches were locked up. We prayed on our little knees by our beds every night, dressed in matching cotton nightgowns with tiny pink flowers and lace around the neck, phony frocks of normality. We prayed for the miracle of food, because it didn't take long for us to find hunger trailing our shadows. Our new confinement was torture compared to the freedom we had learned to exploit in Saint-Servan, and we didn't behave quite as docilely as in the past. Even Arthur raised his hands in despair at our rambunctiousness while secretly happy to see us all in such good health. Although our time in Paris seemed an eternity, it lasted only four weeks. Good news came before long.

Through a stroke of luck, a friend of a friend mentioned to Papa he knew of a tiny village in the mountains near Clermont-Ferrand, in the Massif Central, in south-central France. His suggestion was vague. There was a sort of girls' boardinghouse with a hazy reputation he could not pinpoint. Inquiries were made and satisfied my parents; they did not have the luxury of time to search much longer.

In mid-October, before another devastating winter could grasp us, we were packed once more with the same old clothes and bags. Without delay, Maman led us to the Gare de Lyon from which, by train, we were to reach *Les Hirondelles* (the Swallows), the trip supervised by a Catholic priest who needed to return to his parish in the area, as well as by Maman, who was curious about the reputation of *Les Hirondelles*.

The transition that fall of 1942, from Saint-Servan via Paris to Murols, entailed what had become the usual endless train travel with many stops, discomfort, and lack of food and toilets. The checkpoints and inquiries about our papers were endless. The last lap of the trip I barely survived, my head out the window of a van, unable to keep my meager portions down on the twisted mountain road that led up to Murols.

The camp turned out to be simply a mountain summer camp now operating as a year-round refuge for boys and girls until the end of the war. Its slightly marred reputation was due to a young servant girl getting pregnant by a local boy, but both had decamped, and the place was back to normal. There were thirty-five children in residence, and the five of us made it forty boarders. Charlotte, who had returned to Paris with Papa in September 1941, was continuing her studies in Orléans. She was living with her four favorite cousins, children of Papa's oldest brother, André, and thrilled to be rid of her responsibilities toward us.

# 44
## MERCIFUL MOUNTAINS

*Murols is a tiny village in the mountains of the Massif Central near Clermont-Ferrand in Auvergne, central France. Fanny and Bernard are atop the road sign; under it are Elisabeth, Hélène, and our baby sister, Édith. Taken by Papa on his one visit in 1943.*

*M*urols, our destination village, was located in the Puy de Dôme, a large lava dome in a region of dormant volcanoes, cinder cones, and maars. Fields of black rocks, jagged stones, and magma fragments of all sizes covered the ground, harder than rock and tougher than cement. This became our domicile and playground.

If somewhat desolate at eight hundred meters above sea level, the area had its hidden charms. Only one mile to the south, the lovely Lake Chambon, with its black lava stone beach and freezing waters, gave us many opportunities to swim. Within three miles on hard rocky trails demanding Herculean hiking, there were plenty of sights to see: the massive ruins of a thirteenth-century castle, the Jump of the Maiden, where one maiden had committed suicide after a lost love affair, and the Tooth of the Marais—where wolves had attacked bandits, saving the village from pillage and rape—with jagged black rocks jutting out of the rugged terrain.

After three days to get us settled in, Maman took a train back to Paris, satisfied that *Les Hirondelles* was an extremely safe harbor. Far from the sea, way up in the mountains, inaccessible except by four-wheel drive up an impossible road, producing nothing of any value to an encroaching enemy, Maman could tell Papa, "*Ils sont enfin en bonnes mains* (They are at last in good hands)."

As soon as we settled in, we experienced major changes in our lives: separation from each other, adaptation to a noisy orphan camp, different foods, long hikes on mountain trails, and attending *les classes*, a pseudo-alternative for school.

Separation was the most abrupt and challenging situation. Each of us was assigned to a bedroom with kids our own age. At six and a half years old, I had three roommates who were either six or seven. Fanny and Zabeth were also separated and had their own roommates. Édith, just four years old, was placed with the two- to five-year-olds, six little ones living in a nursery all their own. We rarely saw her, as the babies' schedule was different from ours. Bernard was with all the other boys up on the third floor, the equivalent of the American fourth floor. Walk-up, of course.

None of us made close friends in Murols during our stay of twenty months. It was as if the war made us into autonomous beings, unable to form the special bonds required to build a real friendship. We lost track of everyone from that time, except for the owners, the two sisters Mesdemoiselles de Rigny, and their nephew, Jacques, whom we kept in touch with for years.

Different groups also led to different schedules, so we no longer shared the same experiences. My brother's birthday in September threw him into the older eight-to-nine group, paving a path for misery, as he was the youngest and rather small for his age. Zabeth at nine was in his group but of no help. She was a tomboy and often got into trouble. Fanny was fortunate because, at ten years old, she was essentially in an all-girls group. They supported each other and seemed to form real bonds, at least for the time we lived there. My group was for six- and seven-year-olds, and since I was still a relatively quiet child I had no problem falling in line with the routine and discipline.

The second change was attending what they called *les classes.* Two instructors gave these classes, although they weren't trained as teachers. The acidulous Mademoiselle Berthe taught grammar, arithmetic, and social studies for an hour each day. The endearing Monsieur Schnebaum taught art, music, and nature. He was Jewish and happy to be roofed in this no man's land of freedom, far from the Germans. He adored all the children, and we revered him.

Monsieur Schnebaum lived on the third floor, supervising the fourteen boys in three bedrooms. The sewing room, playroom, and nursery, with the six little ones, were on the first floor, also occupied by the two de Rigny sisters, their nephew, Jacques, in his early twenties, a chambermaid, and the cook. On the ground floor were the common rooms used for classes, meals, a little entertainment we created occasionally, and just hanging out. That is where Monsieur Schnebaum taught us old songs and had us write and perform plays. He showed us Chinese shadows by hanging a sheet across the room and shining a light on one of us dancing on the other side. He took us on long hikes. We marched along singing songs and learning the names of trees and plants, finding odd figures in the clouds, living the closest semblance of a childhood we ever had.

Mademoiselle Berthe, convinced that every child had the hidden potential of being a monster, regulated with her hard ruler and pliable bamboo sticks, beating our fingers when our work did not comply with her demands. Monsieur Schnebaum enchanted us with his baton and paintbrushes in his music and art classes. He taught us the beat of music and dance with dozens of songs I still catch myself humming. She viciously whipped bamboo canes across our backs and buttocks when outside on walks, while he picked flowers for us and taught us to whistle like birds. Her demeanor and presence alone scared us, and we all wanted to sit in the back row. He'd give us a free hand to sit anywhere, complimenting our lack of talent in little drawings made with charcoal from the fireplace, wiping our hands with a dirty rag to keep our clothes clean.

Mademoiselle Berthe and Monsieur Schnebaum were complete opposites and lived in such totally different worlds under the same roof that they never even talked to each other. She was born in those mountains and raised nearby, with a total lack of flexibility in body or in spirit. Her eyes were not quite aligned and gave her a look of cruelty through thin, rimmed glasses, which she never removed. She commanded our second floor with twenty girls set up in five bedrooms. She was terrifying, and the only girl who ever stood up to her was Zabeth, who was punished all the time as a result.

Zabeth couldn't help it; without searching for it, she found trouble everywhere. Mademoiselle Berthe would beat her with her sticks and make her go to her room without dinner. She would make Zabeth write on the blackboard one long phrase that would go from the left edge to the right one, something on the order of: "I promise I will never again leave the walking line to the lake, signed, Elisabeth." One hundred times. When the board was filled she'd count the lines, erase, and restart at the top. She had developed a beautiful handwriting and was able to create practically perfectly straight lines from left to right. She knew she did wrong, but it just seemed to be her nature. She wrote her lines, went wild again, was punished again—write, count, erase, repeat.

I'll never understand her need to rebel, but her desire to be the insurgent was unrelenting. To this day it is difficult to imagine that, although she may have improved her handwriting skills, she seemed to forget that corporal punishment awaited every misstep.

One day, having found Mademoiselle's room unlocked, she snuck into it, took all the bamboo sticks, broke them into tiny pieces, went into her bedroom, and threw them out the window. The courtyard below with all the broken pieces made it obvious who the culprit was.

Whatever the cost, Zabeth felt vindicated and carried on with all sorts of mischief. At church she'd put her hand in the collection basket and pull a coin out instead of putting one in! Things like that, innovative sometimes, put her on a blacklist of culprits. Only two boys had the same truant character, but Mademoiselle Berthe did not feel capable of disciplining them the way she did Zabeth—they were fourteen and her height.

Monday to Saturday, from nine to noon, classes were held in a haphazard schedule posted on a blackboard in the hall. Somehow six days a week we all were taught something, but I never figured out how they managed it, nor do I remember a thing I learned except for the songs. There was never any homework, because there were not enough notebooks to go around or any time to complete homework had it been assigned, since our days had set schedules from nine to five.

Our learning was extremely unconventional, with classes held for one or several groups. The only constant, which I treasured, was my own thin green-covered, blue-lined notebook with a printed frame on the cover with two lines: Name and Class. I was heartbroken when it was abandoned on our departure; it was the only thing I ever had there. I missed it for months afterward and later kept every school notebook I ever used for as long as I could.

At noon a big bell pealed outside the kitchen door, and lunch was served to a tumultuous line of kids waiting with empty plates at the kitchen door. We helped set and clear the table. At one o'clock the little ones napped in their nursery, and we were free to do nothing. By three o'clock a group activity was scheduled for the rest of us, always outside unless it was raining.

Sundays we went to Mass in a tiny chapel in the village, but there were no nuns dressed in long black habits with their faces enclosed in a white cowl, there were no hymns to hum, and you couldn't hear the Latin prayers learned by rote. No, there was just an old priest who mumbled through it and dashed off to serve several villages in the mountains, a local altar boy, village people, and our colony of young kids haphazardly gathered there by the forces of war.

Aside from the worn-out clothing we had brought with us, we each received a *tablier*, a blue apron made of a thick blue cotton fabric with a very specific tightly woven pattern. This garment was worn by every woman in the region. With a bib held up by a loop slung behind the neck and two large front pockets, it wrapped comfortably around the waist, like a skirt, down to the knees and tied in the back. That was the only uniform we owned, though all of us refugee children looked pretty much the same, as we were all in dire circumstances, and shorts and T-shirts were the norm. We also had identical haircuts: straight above the shoulders under the earlobe with bangs, shorn once a month by one of the two sisters de Rigny.

We walked in wooden shoes summer and winter and got free coats for the winter through the church charity. All of these were abandoned— the old clothes, the apron, the coat, along with our notebooks—when we left. When we left we had the clothes on our backs, and that was all.

Finally, we had to adapt to the noise and the group meals. Noise began at seven with fighting for bathrooms, finding the right shorts and T-shirt, slamming our wooden clogs down the stairs, and lining up with an empty bowl at the kitchen door for breakfast. The boys were particularly rambunctious, cascading from the highest floor to the lowest in one thunderous avalanche. I cowered in a corner to let them pass. For us, coming from a quiet conservative convent in Brittany, this was pure pandemonium.

Mealtimes, however, surpassed all else in volume and madness. In line, kids would push and shove to get their hot chocolate and slice of bread. They rushed to the dining-room table to sit with their friends. Most of the kids had been at *Les Hirondelles* from the start of the war and didn't try for a minute to have us join their cliques, except for Fanny's sweet group of girls.

We sat on long benches along each side of the dining-room tables. I was extremely shy and always opted for the end of a bench nearest to a window. Maybe Zabeth would come by me, but she was often punished and made to sit facing a wall with the other rebels.

Bernard was trying hard to adjust to a boy's life. He would have seemed a sissy if he had come to sit with me. I could see it in his apologetic eyes when he took a seat elsewhere. I could never quite get used to everybody screaming to each other, looking forward to the abrupt end of the cacophony when a whistle blew for class at nine o'clock. Lunch and dinner were the same boisterous confusion. We had quiet only during classes and when we went to our room at eight, lights out at nine.

The food was vastly different. In the mountains we were supplied mostly with lentils and rough local root vegetables: cabbage, carrots, onions, parsnips, potatoes, rutabagas, salsify, and turnips. Any one of these would be boiled, chopped, and added with salt to a large kettle of cooked lentils, boiled potatoes, or rice, and served one ladle each in a deep dinner plate made of thick white unbreakable ceramic. That was lunch, and that was dinner, sometimes with a piece of meat, boiled, either beef, chicken, or pork, occasionally followed by a fruit if in season, sometimes the treat of a slice of the local cheese, Saint Nectaire.

Dry lentils came in large burlap bags, about ten pounds each, full of little black rocks and debris. Piles of lentils were placed on the long tables covered with newspapers spread over the *toile cirée* (oilcloth), and we'd sit on each side, separating the good lentils from the bad stuff.

Inevitably, some tiny rocks would be missed, so you had to be careful when eating not to break a tooth.

The most demanding physical adjustment was the topography of this region. We were foreigners to mountainous terrain. The steepest climb we'd ever encountered was from the beach up to the convent, a tenth of a mile at the most. But here when we walked, we walked miles each day and there was no flat terrain. We walked five miles to the château, four to the lake; nothing was closer than three miles, all on dirt roads full of stones and pebbles and scraggly dry bushes on the edges.

We walked three miles to Saint Nectaire, a small village renowned for its cheese. The cheese wheels, about nine inches wide and two inches high, were set to mature on wood shelves in a cool cellar. About twice a month, they needed to be "washed" with fresh cow's milk. One day Jacques de Rigny took us there, but only Bernard was allowed to help him in this task.

Arriving in the cellar, Bernard was overwhelmed by the pungent hazelnut-mushroom smell, but Jacques insisted he'd get used to it. Sitting down with a large rubber apron across his knees, Jacques would take a cheese wheel on his lap and wash it with a rag soaked in the milk. Bernard's task was to give him a fresh rag full of milk, take the used one, rinse it in the pail, and repeat the process until every cheese was done on both sides. As the cheese "grew like a mushroom," this process would help harden the rind and, when ready, off it was shipped to market.

A group of us hung out outside, so a farmer lined us up for a special treat of milk drawn fresh from a cow. His wife milked the cow into a grimy pail. She went off to get a tin cup hanging from a hook on the wall. She plunged it into the steaming milk and passed it on to the first child. When it came to my turn, I took one swallow, gagged, stumbled back a few steps, and threw up. To this day I am incapable of swallowing milk, even the wonderful ice-cold American product.

That winter, sawing wood for the fireplace became a daily chore and Jacques, who had taken him under his wing, asked Bernard to stack the wood neatly onto the large woodpile that rested against the outer wall of the small courtyard at one side of the house. He was the only one permitted to be nearby, as the saw was gigantic. Bernard was careful to stand away while the machine was on, and would pick up logs only once he got the signal. Bernard was happy to have a guardian all to himself, to stave off the bigger boys who intimidated and bullied him.

When winter came with its winds blowing through the pines, we still took walks, but not as long. We sang songs in the dining room, played group games, followed classes, ate root vegetables, and did not complain. Cold as it was, it never seemed as cold as when we all froze in Paris, covered in curtains and shaking from debilitating diseases. Then, unexpectedly, the holiday of Christmas burst on the scene, with a series of new revelations in our lives.

*Taken by Papa in August 1943, this is a rare photo of the six of us Gaillet children together. Elisabeth is in the traditional long white dress and veil borrowed for her Day of Confirmation. Bernard and I received our First Communion. Édith at five had to wait another two years for this special Catholic rite.*

# 45
## REVELATIONS AND INJUSTICE

Christmas was hardly a holiday to celebrate, but it was the first I can remember, and I will never forget it.

A few of the children received something from distant parents, and I was blessed to get a package wrapped in brown paper from Tante Thérèse, my godmother, who was still in Marseille. I had just turned seven years old on December 1, 1942, and this was the very first gift I ever received that was my own! I was tense and excited.

On opening it, I found a gorgeous multicolored *toupie*, a humming-top, with a bright-red wood handle. When I pushed down on the handle the top would spin on the floor and hum different notes depending on the speed of the turn. It was extraordinary! I had never seen anything like it. I was overjoyed and sat on the floor of my room with several girls around me, admiring this miraculously beautiful toy. I had trouble pushing the handle down hard enough, so an older girl showed me how. We'd burst into fits of laughter and clap our hands every time someone succeeded. I was living the most exhilarating moment of my life, and I was sharing it, surrounded with friends.

Suddenly, Mademoiselle Berthe stormed into the room and screamed that we were making too much noise. She gasped when she saw the beautiful *toupie* on the floor. It was as if it were a grenade. She pushed through the girls sitting around, grabbed the *toupie*, and stomped out of the room, confiscating it. I never saw it again.

I cried and cried for days, inconsolable. Where was Maman to complain to? Where was Charlotte to march down to city hall and convince someone that a great injustice had been committed? I couldn't even cling to Bernard as I always had when my nightmares had gotten too close to reality. I could no longer even pretend Maman was there to console me, her touch such a distant memory. This abominable injustice has stayed with me all these years.

My first Christmas, my only one, shattered and destroyed in one gesture, leaving a trail of festering anger in a little girl.

Life went on like this week after week and suddenly, in the first week of August 1943, Papa, Maman, and Charlotte arrived, unannounced, on bicycles. What an amazing apparition! We were struck dumb at their presence. We just stood there while the Demoiselles de Rigny welcomed them effusively and pushed us forward to say hello. Édith had just turned five in May. She looked up at this beautiful smiling lady reaching for her, extended her hand, did a slight curtsy as she had been taught, and said, "Bonjour, Madame." Maman burst into tears.

We all cried. We cried some more when Maman told us that Arthur, our wonderful faithful butler, had suffered a stroke and had to go back with Léontine to their village to live with a nephew. They had left us for good, a huge loss for the family. Their absence left a void in our lives. He was eighty-six and she was eighty-two. We cried a lot during that visit; we cried about everything; we cried all the time.

They stayed only ten days, ten days of crying and joy. Their presence and having the whole family together brought so much sunshine into our lives in spite of all our tears. We took a hike to a favored nearby site where the medieval Château de Murols sat atop a hill three miles north of us. The remains of outer and inner walls still stood, but the inner floors and roofs had collapsed and disappeared. Several stone stairways were still in place, as well as the moat that surrounded the periphery.

Because it was a tourist attraction, its drawbridge had been maintained in working condition, and those stairways enabled us to climb to the ramparts. One of those rampart walls was long and narrow and had lost its retaining sides. Traversing its length excited Zabeth, who practically ran across, but Bernard was petrified, fearing he would be blown away.

There is a family picture of our group on that wall taken by Papa. In that photo, Bernard is sitting down in front of the whole family, his juvenile way of protecting himself from some unpredictable wind puff. He finally did make it to the other end when Maman came up behind him and held the back of his collar to steady him across that empty space. Papa took some more photographs on Sunday outside after church. Zabeth made her Confirmation, and Bernard and I made our First Communion, an event that left no impact on any of us, so absorbed were we with our parents.

Papa didn't tell us many stories about the war raging outside our mountains as he used to. He didn't want to spoil his visit with stories about life in the occupied zone, with Paris still under the heel of the Nazis. He saw how faraway we were from it all and realized how little he knew about any of us now.

"Let them be safe," he said to Maman. "Let them be safe and enjoy this. There will be time enough for the truth later, after the war, later."

We all went swimming in the cold waters of Lac Chambon, had a picnic or two, went to buy fresh cheese in Saint Nectaire, went on excursions through the old château, walked everywhere in an inseparable cocoon. This short visit was the only time we saw my parents and Charlotte during those twenty months in Murols. All were becoming strangers in my mind. I had lost the warmth of Maman's smile.

I remember crying a lot and saying very little, listening to everyone and staring at Maman, thinking I might never see her again. I had that horrible feeling again, those overpowering nightmares that Maman and I would be covered in blood and die together in a deep hole, with Bernard looking down and calling to us. Their visit was memorable, tinged with fear and joy. Then they were gone, and I cried myself to sleep every night.

# PART ELEVEN

# 46
## FOOD AND FLOOD

*M*y parents were highly relieved at our good health and our distance from the war. Heading back to Paris, they shed their worries and anxiety. Their bikes were loaded with foods from the market. Across the handlebars, Papa had tied a huge ham and a slab of Saint Nectaire cheese, Maman had her rear baskets full of canned goods and dry staples, and Charlotte had two chickens and eggs.

A truck full of German soldiers, no more than eighteen years old, stopped them near Clermont-Ferrand. Seeing they were poor refugees, the Germans let them go by without questions. A few kilometers north, a black Citroen coming in their direction stopped suddenly and waved them down. Four French FFI (French Resistance) armed with machine guns asked Papa if he'd seen any enemies on their way. Papa pointed south and said yes, less than fifteen minutes ago, over there. They tore out, and several minutes later Papa heard the unmistakable sound of gunfire.

That first day they covered 175 miles, proving that all their bicycling during the war was paying off. The second day they covered the last hundred miles to Paris under beautiful weather, letting Charlotte with her chickens rejoin her cousins in Orléans.

By fall 1943, Maman had excellent control of the gallery, developing amazing skills in the art world, piling up money in the bank, and easily making friends with artists and writers. One of them invited my parents for a weekend at a beautiful estate in Sologne, 125 miles south of Paris.

The old lodge was a welcome getaway from the pressures of living under the scythe of an omnipresent enemy. The openness of the fields, country air, good food, and wine revived their spirits from the moment they arrived.

The planned activity was to dredge one of their fishing ponds to remove the muddy sediment that accumulates at the bottom, a yearly ritual. When there is only a little water left on the bottom, the carp concentrate in the center and are caught with nets by local farmers. The process is very messy as the carp jump up several feet, splashing mud and water all over. They are separated from the smaller fish and held in large covered pots until returned to fresh waters, where they disappear down deep. The smaller fish are donated to the locals, who come and help for this maneuver, which always turns out to be a country feast.

When some of the carp were offered to her, Maman accepted a good dozen live fish and dropped them in the bathtub, frisky and alive, although they'd been transported in nothing more than wet newspapers in a bucket. Water was scarce. Still, she would leave the cold-water faucet open a tad, excess water dripping out the overflow drain. Sometimes a carp would leap out at night and *clac-clac-clac* on the tiles to their great joy; the carp were alive.

"Long live the carp!" Papa would shout.

One afternoon, the electrician arrived to repair their radio. On entering the library, he found his feet squashing through a water-soaked carpet. A dying carp had gotten stuck on the overflow drain and water had flooded the bathroom and beyond, soon dripping into the apartment underneath theirs. Panic set in with much confusion, as they had never met the occupants. The concierge became the intermediary, determining how much damage to repair, what to replace; after appropriate apologies, a payoff closed the incident, with a couple of fresh carp in the bargain.

How lucky it was that their neighbors were not Germans, thought Papa, as they certainly would have tried to grab our apartment.

Paris in September 1943 was often without electricity, almost without water, and practically without merchants; most stores were now closed due to lack of merchandise. About the only thing to procure on a daily basis was bread. Since they had no coal for cooking, Papa purchased an ingenious camping stove that discharged a little bit of heat when fed with compressed balls of damp newspaper. In twenty minutes they could make a tepid cup of *chicorée*, an ersatz substitute for coffee. Once again, paper to the rescue. Papa and Maman would always joke about Arthur saying, "Why without paper, there would be no coffee!"

They often joined Bon Papa, where his cook, Hortense, would prepare lunch in the little garden behind his ground-floor apartment. Her camping stove was a great deal more impressive than Papa's, bigger, faster, mounted on legs waist high, and using readily available charcoal. Her food supplies, though, were meager and consisted mostly of potatoes and a few vegetables. They agreed to combine their resources. Papa brought the ham and Saint Nectaire and left the prepping to her. Secretly, knowing how voracious Bon Papa could be, he instructed her to be parsimonious with their rations, and these goods lasted through a number of meals.

And so another year went by under the control of the Nazis. Papa and Maman listened to the news of war on the radio and cringed at the destruction of their beautiful country. They never became immune to the disasters surrounding them. They used their bikes to go everywhere. The gallery continued successfully. Papa was able to keep the Germans at bay, keeping their hands off the French paper industry.

We children were safe in the mountains but too far for them to visit us. Knowing we were safe brought them great peace of mind and brought us loneliness. They had no intention of repeating their mistake of bringing us back to Paris. Those days of occupation in Paris remain indelible in our memories, jumbled into one long day of terror, disaster, fear, famine, and unhappiness.

# 47

## CITY OF SQUALLS

*A*round ten o'clock on August 24, 1944, Papa received a phone call from a friend who lived in Vitry-sur-Seine, seven and a half miles south of Notre Dame Cathedral: his town had just been liberated without any fighting!

The next day at lunch with Bon Papa, Hortense, with her customary exuberance, burst into the garden and said, "The French have arrived! *Ils sont lá!*"

Without even saying good-bye, Papa jumped on his bike and dashed off to Place de l'Étoile. He knew if anything was going to happen, it had to be there, the center of Paris with l'Arc de Triomphe, our symbol of liberty. It was almost empty of civilians, but two long columns of French tanks ran all the way to the horizon, one on the north side down the Avenue de la Grande Armée, the other to its left down Avenue Foch. Papa's heart jumped.

"To the devil with precautions!" he thought. He dropped the bike against one of the fences bordering the beautiful apartment buildings around the Place and ran to stand under the Arc de Triomphe. From there he had an incredible 360° view, the convergence of twelve magnificent avenues.

He stood on the inside of the northwest pillar. Arriving cautiously, onlookers began to gather around him under the Arc. All stood quietly, mesmerized, the air still, no more than maybe thirty people, hardly anyone around the sidewalks beyond. Calming down, Papa looked around with more focus, noticing the heaving rumble of motors.

Suddenly, he stopped breathing. A little to the east, hiding in the roundabout between Avenue de la Grande Armée and Avenue Carnot was a huge German Panzer tank. Papa wondered if the French saw this.

"Someone must warn them!" he thought. But how could they? The soldiers were all concealed inside their turrets and were unapproachable. He waited.

Suddenly, the French tanks rumbled and began to roll forward, slowly, ever so imposing, a great moment of decision. The tanks were a gift from the Allies to the army of Général Leclerc to let the French savor the idea of liberating Paris.

Everyone was crying in silence. Papa's heart was in his throat; he couldn't have uttered a word. They watched this slow-motion thrilling moment of the French liberating Paris. Their beautiful city would be theirs again.

*Paris Libre!* Could it be?

The detonation of a cannon made them all jump for cover, pressing into the wall. The cannonball landed on the German Panzer, from which erupted a white flag, followed by seven men with their arms up in the air, climbing out onto the pavement. They lined up, hands high, and faced the Arc.

It became quiet again. People were numb, no one talking, rumbling motors the only sound. The Germans stood next to their tank. They had no place to go.

The line of French tanks continued flowing slowly onto the Place de l'Étoile and began to go around the Arc de Triomphe, circling from the north around to Papa's left, heading south. That's when he noticed another hidden German Panzer, two blocks south of the second column, on the roundabout by Avenue Kléber. It was standing still, almost in front of the Hotel Majestic, which had harbored many of the administrative offices of the Germans.

As he stared at it, that second Panzer tank opened fire on the French tanks entering the Place de l'Étoile. War was at his feet. This was the end. He would be killed as Paris was being reborn. Lucid for a moment, Papa could appreciate the four solid columns supporting the Arc, harboring the hypnotized onlookers.

And then the first Panzer tank exploded, the soldiers standing in front of it thrown to the ground, probably dead. A following salvo hit the other tank, which caught fire, incinerating the soldiers inside. The trees nearby were also incinerated. Papa and the people by him felt the heat on their faces, but none of them could move or say a word.

Shots followed. Papa heard them coming from farther away, from different places. Then he saw a thick cloud of smoke rising slowly toward a deep-blue sky. Down to the south, Le Grand Palais, a magnificent Beaux-Arts building, was ablaze. Shots continued here and there. It was impossible to pinpoint their origin or their targets. Sporadic fighting erupted in various districts.

The captive onlookers under the Arc, protected by its thick pillars, could not look at each other, couldn't talk, would die if they moved.

Suddenly, the woman crouched next to Papa darted out, terrified, and ran off to cross the huge Place de l'Étoile. Screaming, she ran toward the French tanks when a stray bullet from a rooftop blasted into her chest and she fell, knocked over backward, twenty yards from where he stood. He saw the red blood spreading on her white blouse, her navy skirt astray on her hips, torn stockings (she wore stockings, how did he even notice that?), her head turned in that certain angle of death.

Nobody could move. The tanks were now slowly rolling toward the southern end, the beginning of the Champs-Elysées that glides down to La Concorde.

A few French soldiers appeared from nowhere with machine guns at the ready and rushed to attack the Hotel Majestic. In less than fifteen minutes, a dozen Germans came out, hands in the air, waving white napkins. Two French soldiers lined them up and marched them by, so close to Papa he could see how young they were, so afraid.

One put a hand in his pocket as if to pull out a pistol, and simultaneously a clamor of gunshots riffled through them, and all lay dead on the ground. Papa hated blood, he hated death, he hated war, he hated Nazis, but he couldn't help but stare at these poor boys, dead on the pavement like the corpses of WWOne.

Three days later, the news ran through Paris that Général de Gaulle, his entourage, and the leaders of the Resistance were to march down the Champs-Elysées. Thousands of Parisians rushed out to join them.

This time Papa left his bicycle at home, knowing that sheer luck had saved it from being stolen or destroyed the other day. He ran to see a crowd growing from all directions. With the hundreds growing to thousands, Papa joined the formation toward the front of the crowd, which kept going to the quays, over the Pont de Notre Dame and onto the plaza in front of the cathedral. Many of those in front were able to follow the leaders into the cathedral, where a choir and orchestra were miraculously assembled to sing a *Te Deum Laudamus* (Thee, O God, We Praise), the solemn music bringing everyone to their knees in tears.

The crowd was intense and quiet inside, but once released it became a free-for-all of joy and celebration, wails and hallelujahs echoing everywhere, people waving little French and American flags. Thousands of people were dancing and kissing, crying hysterically at the release of years of emotions and sadness, frustration and famine. It was scary and uproarious at the same time.

Papa had been reunited with a few scattered friends, and they marched away, unable to stop blubbering, wiping their eyes. It was really happening, they were free!

They were comparing notes on what they all saw and heard. Everyone had a different version, but all agreed on the bottom line: freedom was here to stay. As they headed past the Musée du Louvre, shots rang out close by. They couldn't believe it, just when happiness was within reach, they could be killed at the last minute.

Most of the people who had been around them ran as soon as they heard the first shots, across Rue de Rivoli to duck for cover under its arcades. Papa's group had been somewhat farther back and was on the wrong side of the street, in open air without shelter. The best they could do was squat behind a bench and a lamppost. Apparently, rogue shooters from up high were aiming into crowds, shooting anywhere, indiscriminately. *La guerre des toits* (the war of the rooftops) had begun over their heads.

Occasionally a lull would prevail, and someone would peel off the edge and run away, and then another. The small crowd was thinning; Papa waited, profoundly disturbed, undecided. A young woman, leaning by him, said, "I am so scared." Remembering the death of the woman who had run at l'Étoile, he urged her to remain where she was. "Don't move, absolutely don't move!" Papa said. "It'll be over soon."

Just then a young man left their little group. A bullet from the roof nearest to them ripped into his throat. He fell without a sound, remained still on the deserted street, his arms extended in the form of a cross, and died instantly.

None of them moved for the longest time while gunfire rang haphazardly in different directions. And then it stopped. Papa counted the minutes into the silence and finally could tell it was over. They could resume their day as traffic began to roll, and people quietly headed home. But he just stood there, frozen.

An ambulance stopped, a jeep with a big red cross. A priest came out and knelt by the deceased, said a loud prayer, and formed a majestic sign of the cross over his body. The medics grabbed a stretcher, threw the dead into the jeep, and took off. More ambulances followed, picking others who lay on the ground, some moaning, some not. Trucks arrived with soldiers, who canvassed buildings one after the other, sometimes coming out with a prisoner.

Papa stood there overwhelmed, watching it all, his eyes stinging from the sun and the tears. Eventually he made his way to the arcades of Rue de Rivoli, unable to recall how he got there. That night at seven fifteen, Général de Gaulle entered the town hall and signed the peace agreement. Peace was here to revive the City of Lights.

After these memorable days, life progressively stabilized. Street cleaners swept debris with their odd brooms made of twigs tied with twine to a tree branch for a handle. Electricity and water were doled out more frequently, clocks swung back to regular daytime hours, and café terraces filled with relaxed civilians drinking bottomless demi-tasses of espresso, smoking cigarettes and reading newspapers.

Papa tried to pick up various odds and ends of the business and went to meet the new ministers at the Chamber of Commerce, but their industry was quite paralyzed because the transportation systems were so disrupted. Some six thousand bridges had been destroyed all over France, interrupting train and car traffic in many parts of the country. He would sit at his desk and pray.

And into the night he would wail and continue crying with Maman, mingling their tears they would beg God to return their children to them safe and sound. *"Ah, mon Dieu, où sont nos enfants?* Oh, God, where are our children?"

# 48

## FIRE AND LOSS

While Paris had been liberated, the war was not quite over yet for several weeks. There were some haphazard night bombardments that missed any targets of note, and stray Germans still tried to kill a few French. However, now, the French could concentrate on their individual lives and families.

In early September 1944, a messenger on a bicycle arrived from Blendecques and told Bon Papa some terrible news. While most of the family properties in the North were somewhat intact, our new house, used as the German headquarters throughout the war, had been burned to the ground on the day of the Liberation.

In shock, Bon Papa called my parents to come have dinner with him that evening. He told them the news in his most dignified way. Maman fell into tears but, curiously enough, Papa felt nothing. Having witnessed such prodigious events, he couldn't react to one more. Neither surprise nor regret could touch him at the time.

Details were sad and true. As the villagers at Blendecques learned of the Liberation, the German officers had piled up in jeeps and fled the house, without a word to their subordinates. Finding out they had been abandoned, and knowing that soon they'd be made prisoners, the remaining soldiers went to the cellar to have a wild time with the wine and liquor left behind. Drunk with the despair of their defeat, they looked for vengeance. They grabbed cans of gasoline, spilled it all over the house, threw in a match, and burned it down.

Firemen arrived but were held back by the armed drunkards menacingly waving their guns. A few local women were behind them laughing, women who had become their mistresses who would soon be forced to parade through the streets nearly naked with their heads shaved, who would be called *collabos horizontales* (horizontal collaborators). Their pictures would be all over the papers, anointed in shame, but for now they were nasty to our neighbors trying to put out the fire.

The fire raged on, nothing was saved, only the strong red-brick chimneys were left standing, symbols of destruction, symbols of liberty.

The loss of everything we owned played a large role in Papa's future decisions. His grandfather in 1870, and he in 1944, had lost their homes and belongings following German invasions. It was time for him to change our destiny, to keep his children from becoming victims of the same fate.

*Our beautiful house was burned to the ground the day of the Liberation.
Nothing was saved but the outer walls and the chimney. The Nazi officers had
left overnight, abandoning their young soldiers to fate. Papa took this photo a
few weeks after the disaster; he wouldn't let Maman see it for months.*

# 49
## LIBERATION

*E*cstatic with France's new freedom, Maman couldn't wait to get us all back to Paris, to have the family under one roof, to be sure we were all still alive after so many tribulations. She knew repatriating us to Paris would not be an easy feat, but she jumped into the fray.

All of France was on the move. Thousands of refugees like us were trying to get back home. Public transportation was at a near standstill because of destroyed train stations, bombed bridges, inaccessible roads, and lack of gasoline. The demarcation line was dismantled in record time, police posts and signs torn down in glee and burned in bonfires. Main roads were reopened as fast as possible. Civilians of all backgrounds and workers of all levels were put to work by the government to sort out the most important repairs to be done first. Determined refugees found their way home as best they could, many to discover only ruins. Still, it was their land, their roots, and they would rebuild.

Questioning many of her contacts for information on organizations for repatriation, Maman quickly found out that she would have to get us back herself. Going from bureaucratic officials to school and church services, she found a Catholic priest who took it upon himself to gather Parisian children around Auvergne and accompany them back to the city. She glued herself to him for a tortuous trip down to Clermond-Ferrand, where they stayed in a semi-abandoned army depot with dozens of others in the same catchall, trying to figure out how to organize their mission.

Through local churches and city halls, several towns with colonies of young refugees needing escorts were alerted, and responses piled up quickly. Within a week, they had a group of about six dozen kids of all ages, four other adults, and themselves. They decided to start the move without delay, first gathering everyone at the army depot where they had set up base. Of course, transportation was the major problem. It could only be solved step by step, stop by stop, destination by destination, and it was a nightmare for the entire four-hundred-mile trip from Murols to Paris.

With no other way to get off the top of our mountain, we left the refuge of Murols walking. We walked for days without letup, through a large forest, through plains with sheep grazing peacefully, through villages with dogs barking, sleeping in the woods at night.

We reached the nearest town bisected by a road sloping downhill. We marched like little soldiers, sang all the songs taught to us by Monsieur Schnebaum, who was marching with us, as he planned to go home, a Jewish survivor of World War II, a living miracle. Later, before going on to find out if any of his family was still alive, he visited us in Paris.

We were lightheaded, we had no luggage, and we sang rain or shine. I only carried my doll, Thérèse, because the only toy I ever got, my *toupie*, had been stolen and lost forever. It was warm in early September, so we wore our T-shirts and our navy-blue shorts and tied our *pulls marins* around our waist. We clapped our wooden shoes on the dirt roads, focusing ahead.

At a wider road, open trucks driven by local farmers picked us up and took us to the army depot, where we finally ran into Maman, who was standing outside in tears. She had wanted to come to Murols, but was persuaded that to wait here was better and faster. Our reunion was one of jubilation. It was the first time back together for months. There she stood, her dress dirty, her face muddied, her hair a mess—so unlike her, yet I knew her right away.

"Maman, Maman!" I saw her first against the crowd. There she was. I was petrified I would not recognize her after such a long time. Hesitantly I waved, but she was looking somewhere else. The sky cast a spotlight on her worried expression. She was so beautiful. Her face struck my heart; I couldn't stop crying. I began to yell for her, "Maman! Maman!" I ran to her, running as hard as my tired little legs could carry me, bumping into people, losing a wooden shoe.

I screamed louder, "Maman!" unable to reach her in the crowd. Then my other shoe fell off just as she turned to see me.

I dropped my dolly, racing barefoot now as she ran to us. Bernard, in quickstep behind me, grabbed my doll from the dirt, Fanny and Zabeth struggling to follow, pulling Édith with them. We were alive, and we were together. The forceful impact of this reunion will never fade.

At the train station, many other groups of youths met us, grown by word of mouth to many more than those who had signed up. When a train came, we filled up three wagonloads, almost two hundred, packed tighter than boxed cigarettes. Then began the torment of going north.

After the initial euphoria, we chugged along languidly. Stopped at a bridge destroyed by bombs, we got off the train and crossed the obstacle on foot. If a shallow river, we waded across, drinking some of the water in our cupped hands. If too deep, we clambered on small boats rowed by locals, back and forth, six or twelve at a time, a slow process. Whatever it was, we went over it, under it, around it, and found or waited for another train on the other side. We scrambled on, until everyone was on board.

One crossing could take two hours, sometimes more, gathering those who were sick, who were crying, who could hardly stand. The priest, Maman, the other adults would scour nearby bushes and fields to make sure no one was left behind.

Sometimes, somebody would drop some food in our hands, a piece of bread, an apple. We ate it. If we weren't completely constipated, we relieved ourselves in bushes and wiped ourselves with leaves. We urinated underneath ourselves on the train, unable to move. We chugged to the next burned-out bridge, torn-up rails, walking whenever there were no wheels. Our skin chafed between our thighs, irritated by foul moisture.

Finally, five days later, after four hundred miles of harrowing trials, we reached Paris, bedraggled, exhausted, and filthy. With these last four hundred miles, we ended our family exodus, our travails zigzagging France, going to the seashore, to the big city, to the mountains, and finally landing in Paris for good. We had covered 3,755 kilometers (2,338 miles) during those four years of war. We had lost everything, including the treasure of our youth.

*Disastrously unkempt hair shows this must have been taken soon after we arrived from the mountains, but matching dresses show that Maman wanted us to have one clean outfit. Top: Elisabeth (L) and Fanny; bottom: Hélène, Édith, and Bernard. September 1944.*

# 50

## DELIVERANCE

Vaguely remembering the apartment, we all wanted to crowd into the one big bedroom again, but Maman had better ideas. She and Papa had the master suite, Bernard got his own room, and I shared one with Édith. Fanny and Zabeth had another.

Back from Orléans, Charlotte got the big bedroom so her cousins could visit frequently. I was fascinated by the large closet with flat double doors, the inside of which Charlotte decorated with colorful empty packs of American cigarettes, Camels with Turkish blend, Lucky Strike with the red target, Chesterfields with soldiers. She picked them up in the gutters on her way to and from school, along with half-smoked butts American soldiers tossed out, collecting the smelly tobacco and making her own cigarettes with tiny packs of crinkly papers that I coveted just for the feel of them. Truly emancipated at eighteen, she was smart and individualistic, bicycling to the Lycée Cours Dupanloup, where she passed her baccalauréat in philosophy with high marks and then entered the Sorbonne.

My parents had us embrace a new governess, Mademoiselle Fremaux, with curly blond hair and a permanent smile, immediately nicknamed Mazelle. Now that Arthur and Léontine were gone, Mazelle did everything for us. She shopped and cooked, she sewed and cleaned, and she taught us to roller skate on the endless marble sidewalks of the Trocadéro. So dedicated, so patient, so open and fun, Mazelle, coming to us in her twenties, an only child bereft of parents, was a God-given gift and became part of us, even coming to America, where she settled for good after we were all grown up.

Zabeth broke the lock on the big armoire in the sewing room, and we were deluged with beautiful new toys that Madame Tatiana had bought for her daughter Francine, who had never had a chance to play with them, as they lived in New York. This time our parents let us have the toys, figuring there was no use in keeping them from us who had had none for four years.

Bernard, now ten, was accepted at an all-boys school, Lycée Janson-de-Sailly, four blocks north and one to the left on Rue de la Pompe, a fifteen-minute walk. He adapted quite well after living with all those boys in Murols and strengthened his body by walking back and forth every day with a little brown leather schoolbag strapped to his back.

Fanny (twelve and a half), Elisabeth (eleven), Édith (five), and I (eight) were all sent to the Sisters of the Assumption, up one block and to the right on Rue de Lübeck, an all-girls school. I adored the nuns and fell into a endless ritual of learning. I loved every subject, each lesson. I wrote little stories and drew sketches of animals and flowers and plants. Maman never told me to write smaller to save space, we had all the paper we could possibly want now, and—I do have to say it—the luxury of real toilet paper, though it was still horrible, pale-brown crinkly, thin, and nonabsorbent compared to what we have now.

My greatest happiness was to be alone in the library, where I could close the doors and bury myself in the mysteries of books. There, amid grown-up books penned by André Malraux, Marguerite Yourcenar, Jean-Paul Sartre, and Simone Weil, which I perused but did not understand, I discovered treasures that molded my love of reading. *Vol de Nuit* (*Night Flight*) by Antoine de Saint-Exupéry (*Le Petit Prince* came later); *Le Bal* (*The Ball*), a short novel about a mistreated daughter and the revenge of a teenager by Irène Némirovsky, which shocked me with its characters no older than Charlotte (Némirovsky's book *Suite Française* was lost around that time and rediscovered much later); and Georges Siménon, just beginning his prolific career as a writer of detective stories with Commissaire Maigret, writing humorous short stories in questionable magazines I probably should never have discovered.

Many books were beyond my age, but by concentrating one paragraph at a time, rereading chapters, trying to figure out what they were saying, I was able to begin to understand the power of words and the magic of the imagination printed on paper. I didn't just read books—I devoured them. My favorite magazine was *Historia,* found on a low shelf, with all its stories about the history of France with pictures, maps, and details that never sated my curiosity. On seeing how avid I was for more, Maman subscribed me to *Historia* in 1945 and for thirty years after that.

That winter promised to be calmer and easier than the previous ones we'd spent on the edge of freezing, famine, and disease. We became Parisians by default, and our lives turned for the better. Although coal was still scarce, Papa was able to get some from one of his factories. The manager would call to say he had some "dark cardboard goods to drop off." In the evening a small truck would deliver several fat burlap bags, enough to feed our central heating system frugally. Instead of German boots slamming the sidewalks, we had the laughter of American soldiers, who would throw sticks of Juicy Fruit gum at us if we popped out the door.

All was going well with our readjustments when, at the end of October, Fanny complained of some pain. She had difficulty breathing, and it hurt if she coughed. She took to her bed with aspirin and hot tea but could hardly swallow. Maman found it difficult to wake her up the next morning. Her voice was weak and raw, she had thick mucus dripping from her nose, and her face was flushed hot. Some kind of rare illness was grabbing hold of her, and Maman begged the doctor to come right away. The diagnosis was disastrous.

Somber as if he were announcing a death, the doctor said Fanny had contracted a terrible case of highly contagious diphtheria and required immediate quarantine to avoid an epidemic. He explained she must be treated immediately, or she could choke and die of asphyxiation in a matter of days, even hours. There was only one remedy, available only from the Institut Pasteur: an antitoxin vaccine. He called for it.

Charlotte immediately jumped on her bike to pick it up but soon called from the hospital. "Maman!" she screamed into the phone. "They have some vaccine, but they have it only for their patients staying at the hospital! They are full of sick people. They have only one bed available. Maman, can you speak to the doctor here, he wants to talk to you about Fanny!"

That very evening, November 1, 1944, All Saints Day, Fanny, gravely ill and almost delirious, was run by ambulance to the hospital, quarantined in the only empty hospital bed. She was given a strong dose of antitoxin, which was repeated on a daily basis. After a week of excellent care, she was safe, and my parents' anxiety abated. Maman told us that in the epidemics of the past, this illness had been referred to as "the strangling angel of children." She promised us Fanny would recover.

This frightened me to the core. I remembered the tsunami of dangers we had evaded for four years and now, in peace, Fanny could die, and so could we by catching that sickness. I was only eight, and I was certain it would be impossible to ever get to ten years old.

The nuns at Pasteur were dedicated and knowledgable nurses. Also very pious: every evening they opened the doors onto the hallways so all the residents could recite the rosary together. *Pater Noster qui es in cælis, Ave Maria gratia plena* would echo through the halls before lights out as a nun called the first phrase to each prayer out loud. The open doors would carry prayers and contagious diseases from one patient to the other, their immune systems already weakened by what they had.

Papa found it strange that in an institute dedicated to eradicating bacterial diseases, there was so little attention paid to the most rudimentary rules of quarantine. I guess the nuns placed a little more faith in God than Papa could muster at that point. Fanny was kept under surveillance for three months before returning home, limp in Papa's arms, the week before her thirteenth birthday, February 19, 1945.

My parents made sure we knew about the war now that newsreels regurgitated the worst of the films that had been taken by news photographers in all corners of the war front. Every Saturday afternoon, after our morning classes, we saw war pictures I shall never forget: the blitz of London in September 1941 for fifty-seven consecutive nights; groups of refugees struggling on the roads and falling into the gutters; desperate families trying to pass the demarcation line; arrests at train stations and cattle cars full of terrified people; the Nazis laughing at the Jews wearing a yellow Star of David on their chests; the Jews forced to dig long ditches, then line up in front of them to be shot dead and fall over on top of each other, the guards kicking their bodies into the ditch. Caught with Nazis, women with shaved heads were paraded half-naked through the streets as *collabos horizontales,* many shot by infuriated Frenchmen.

We were spared nothing. The cinema was always packed with parents and children alike. Everybody wanted to attest to the atrocities of the war. The slightest image of the war I see today brings back a nightmare full of those scenes indelibly imprinted on my mind.

Maman would often take me to her gallery on Rue des Saints Pères, because she liked my quiet presence. A bus line took us straight from Place d'Iéna to the corner of the street on the quay, and I would saunter to number three. With an air of complicity, she would say I was the only one who could help for what she needed done. For me it was like entering a tomb of secrets. I breathed in deeply the smell of oil paint that pervaded the rooms from fresh works dropped off by artists. I organized piles of drawings and lithos, cleaned up the little bathroom, put out the garbage, making sure all papers had been ripped up in little pieces. Being too short, I couldn't wash the front windows, but I could sweep the floors and the sidewalk and change the water in the little vase of flowers she kept on her desk.

Maman taught me how to frame artwork, holding the mat just so, tapping little nails onto the sides to hold glass and picture in place. Two eye screws had to be tightened on each side in the back, then a wire run in a special way to hold the picture safely on the wall. We would save new artworks in the little room up in the back, the room where the Jewish artist had lived for months. She spoke very little about him. I looked for signs of his existence, for a thread of his life, but found nothing. I tried to smell the cigarette smoke, but it had vanished into thin air. His presence was a void that revealed nothing. The furniture had been removed, the desk transformed with a large plywood board into a worktable for framing. Even the ghost of his life was gone forever. It was unnerving, disappointing.

One day Maman came home thrilled. Someone had given her two tickets to the opera. Papa was away as he so often was, so she asked me to go with her. It was my tenth birthday, December 1, 1945, and she couldn't think of a gift that would be more appropriate than taking me to see *La Veuve Joyeuse* (The Merry Widow), an Austrian operetta by Franz Lehar.

A new horizon beyond reading opened my mind with those colorful lacy costumes floating on stage, a dream world of singing and dancing, all for me in the eighth row aisle seat. Ecstatic and mesmerized, this discovery formed the embryo of a lifelong love of theater and opera that I've enjoyed year after year.

Mazelle became my confidante, and I shared all my experiences with her: the magnificent opera, the shocking newsreels, school discoveries in every class, and wanting to roll up cigarettes with Charlotte. I made her swear she'd never tell about the chewing gum I'd stick on my bedpost at night and pick up again in the morning, or the gum I chewed in class that a nun made me throw out the window, which I retrieved among pebbles in the courtyard during recreation. Mazelle and I shared many dreams about the future. We talked about Papa's missions to America for de Gaulle to buy and sell paper. She swore she'd never go to that forsaken country of redskins, where they shot you with arrows. She said she wanted to stay with us in Paris forever. How little we know about our future.

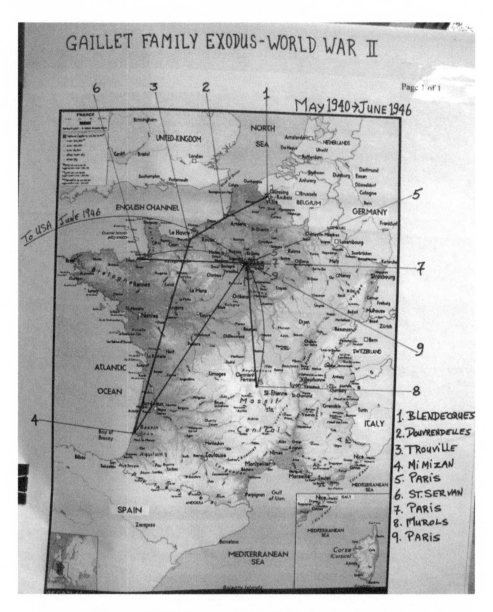

*We covered 3,755 kilometers (2,338 miles) during four years, in a country no larger than Texas, often under extreme duress.*

# 5 1
## A New Beginning

*Papa, with his cigarette ready for a light and his briefcase covered with travel tags, enters the portals to freedom. He will have us all emigrate and become Americans.*

*B*y early 1946, we began to see changes in Papa caused by all his trips to the United States. He slowly switched from smoking Gauloises to Camels. He wore a navy-blue cashmere sweater that winter and brought Maman a box full of nylon stockings. We received care packages of Spam. It took over our pantry; we wanted Spam every day. He'd pull gadgets out of his pockets that we raved over: little key chains with dangling doodads, pencil sharpeners, globes glittering with Santa and snow, shiny bracelets and necklaces, miniature playing cards, magic tricks, comic books. Before we knew it, we each had our own little American treasure trove. When he would leave, we would all lean out the windows and wave au revoir as he called, "What shall I bring back for you?"

"Chewing gum!" we would scream.

The future came suddenly in March 1946, when Papa returned from his third mission to the United States, where he had spent quite a few months. As Papa was a top expert in the paper business with good contacts overseas, de Gaulle had named him emissary abroad for the French paper industry. His missions were to build up trade with the allies and expand import and export overseas.

Remembering some basic school English, Papa had been on extended trips to New York, Washington, DC, Oregon, and California since the Liberation. He had had to surmount quite a few obstacles on these trips but had managed to obtain some propitious contracts that would form the base of successful interchanges between the two countries. While some Americans didn't care to deal with Europe at all, Papa was crazy about the United States, the people, the freedom, and the expansiveness of the country—he loved everything about it. Deep down it no longer appealed to him to continue in a place where suffering was the prefix to his every thought. As well, yet another negative faced him: Tatiana's lawyer contacted him about reclaiming the apartment. Although he knew the law gave him the right to reside there until he himself made the decision to leave, there was no question of staying in Paris much longer. He was losing his taste for all things French and was enchanted with the new world across the Atlantic.

Papa became particularly attracted to an extremely smart and savvy German Jew, Charles Hartig, same age, forty-two, who had immigrated to the United States with his family in 1939 and knew the paper business in depth. Charles persuaded Papa that for a German Jew and a French Catholic to set up an import-export paper business in New York City was the key to their future and a guaranteed success. Hartig had all the contacts in the Unites States and Canada, Papa in France and Europe. This became the foundation for the new firm, Gaillet & Hartig, at 250 Park Avenue, New York City, which they formed in June 1946. It was, indeed, extremely successful until they sold it in the seventies to a huge conglomerate.

However, while Papa could see his future clearly, he had one major hurdle to overcome: convincing Maman. To date, his life had been full of struggles, but he trusted he could find a way to overcome the difficulties facing them if only he could secure her accord. He wasn't sure how to convince her.

Maman was distraught at the idea of losing her gallery, her artists, her world of friends and relatives. She feared the language barrier, having never learned a word of English. She was equally unenthusiastic about building a new house or remodeling some old family property her father offered us in the North. She adored Paris and couldn't imagine any other life.

When I look back, her biggest concern was sort of funny: she was worried about finding appropriate husbands for her five daughters! Like Germany, our homeland had lost thousands of young men, future husbands, on the front. She feared it would be impossible to find proper husbands in France and even less likely in a foreign land. She was hopelessly confused from the few American films she had seen, and she was worried about us being swept away by strange men on horseback in a wild country full of cowboys and Indians.

Their many discussions in the closed library went on late into the night. I could hear them whispering carefully so as not to be heard by us.

"If we don't make it," Papa promised, "we can always come back. Your father will always welcome us back. He would give us some property in Blendecques. We could build a new house or maybe get an apartment here in Paris…" His voice trailed off.

Finally, Maman succumbed to Papa's deep desire to nurture our futures on the shores of his newfound country.

On Friday, June 13, 1946, we made history: we were the first family of eight members to fly across the Atlantic Ocean.

We landed safely at La Guardia Airport in New York City, thanks to Trans World Airlines, but truly it was a miracle. In those days, the North Atlantic route from Paris to New York included refueling stops in Shannon, Ireland, and Gander, Newfoundland. During the first leg of our trip, the airplane lost the use of one of its starboard engines while over the English Channel and landed on three engines in Shannon. After an eight-hour delay for repairs, we took off again toward Gander.

About midway across the Atlantic, the cabin pressure suddenly failed, forcing the pilots to take the plane below ten thousand feet. However, at that altitude, we hit a raging North Atlantic storm. We flew through it, the plane tossing around as if it were a dead leaf torn off a tree during an autumn storm. Sitting by the window and violently sick from the horrible commotion, I could not help comparing my birth in a violent storm and envisioning my death in this one. At certain moments, the plane was no more than several hundred feet above the surface of the ocean. Even the pilots and the cabin crew carried their little barf bags as they tried to keep the passengers calm. Mine was quite useless by then, my stomach empty. We had all donned safety jackets, but they would have been of little use if we had hit the water.

Miraculously, we did make it in one piece to Gander, where the airport had set up emergency procedures for our arrival. Flashing lights and sirens blared as we landed, the crippled airplane maneuvering off kilter as it touched the ground, making a colossal crunching noise I can hear to this day.

Trembling and weak, all passengers were set up on makeshift cots lined up in a huge freezing hangar, away from the public spaces and curious onlookers. Barely aware of the danger we had survived, we dozed and lounged for some twelve hours while crews made the repairs.

The final leg of the flight was uneventful. We landed at LaGuardia in the middle of the night. Press people and photographers awaiting our arrival had been patient. They were there to take a historic picture of the family standing on the landing ramp of the Constellation. Limousines took us to 15 Ocean Avenue, Larchmont Manor, New York.

On its way back to Paris, via the reverse route, our airplane disappeared without a trace halfway across the Atlantic Ocean. This was related to us by reporters who tracked us down in Larchmont. They told us we were truly miraculous new arrivals in their country.

Headlines screamed around the world: "Paris Family Finds Home Waiting," "French Family of Eight Fly to New Larchmont Home—Furnished and Food Stocked," and the best one, "She Finds a Home—and Butter." At last we were safe, and we were home.

*Trans World Airlines turned our flight into history in June 1946. This photo was published in many international newspapers. We had survived the war and were the first large family to fly together across the Atlantic Ocean!*

# EPILOGUE

Much has happened to us since that flight across the Atlantic Ocean. After selling Gaillet and Hartig, my father became president of International Paper and lived in Paris with my mother, traveling all over Europe until they retired in Sarasota, Florida. In good health into their nineties they passed away a year apart in their sleep. My mother need not have worried, we all married displaced Europeans in New York, and at her memorial service there were almost a hundred members of the Gaillet family!

Charlotte married the son of a diplomat, Dimitri Stancioff, a world-renowned biologist and researcher in seaweed. His work took them on scientific trips all over the world. They had five children, most of them living near Camden, Maine, with their own children. She had heart failure and passed away in her mid-eighties; he is well and enjoying his many grandchildren. She and I spent hours reliving our war years, so different that she would often say, "You have your memories, and I have mine."

Fanny married Bernard Guerlain of the perfume family, who worked for many years in the paper business with my father and developed his own importing company, Special Papers. They had eight children, now living from the East to the West Coast, many married with children. Fanny contracted a virus in her midseventies and succumbed to it. Bernard is fine and lives in Rockport, Maine.

Elisabeth married Jean Delavigne and became a successful Real Estate broker while he worked for Coty the French perfume company for years; they had five children who all live in and around Connecticut.

Jean died of a heart attack some twenty years ago; she lives in a lovely retirement home close to her children, who visit often. Quieter now than in her lively years, her passions are Scrabble and card games, at which she wins very often.

Bernard, my beloved brother, died the day before I sent him the first draft of this book a while ago. His loss is hard to accept, I miss him terribly. He was so helpful with photographs and memories, papers from my father, ideas for stories. He leaves two sons and a daughter, all married, each with three children, with whom I remain close.

Édith looks lovely as ever and lives in New Hampshire close to her oldest son, a real estate broker married with two children. Active as mountain guides and photographers, the other two sons live in Switzerland where her husband, Johnny Hadik, now deceased, worked in the banking business for many years. This makes a total of 26 grandchildren for Papa and Maman.

As for me, happily married for 25 years to a retired Danish/Norwegian pharmacist from Brooklyn, William Field de Neergaard, I thrive on being an artist and author, painter and photographer, with a very active life between New York and Naples, Florida.

My first husband, Charles de Barcza, a Hungarian-Italian, passed away many years ago, leaving me with two wonderful, beautiful daughters. Mokus is married to Joseph Szilva, both gifted artists, and together they run a very successful business in New York, *SurfaceStudio.com*. Anne-Charlotte is an executive with Macy's, married to Michael Lohan, an executive with a linen manufacturing company, both often traveling to different points of the world, to Paris, Shanghai and beyond. They have a son, my only grandchild, Matthew Devitt Lohan, at twenty a musician, artist, and world traveler, who will soon graduate from the College of Charleston, already following in my footsteps of a creative life and a free spirit.

Made in United States
North Haven, CT
07 October 2022

25162572R00178